Twayne's United States Authors Series

Sylvia E. Bowman, *Editor*

INDIANA UNIVERSITY

Frederick Goddard Tuckerman

FREDERICK GODDARD TUCKERMAN

By SAMUEL A. GOLDEN

Wayne State University

 104

Twayne Publishers, Inc.   ::   New York

MANUFACTURED IN THE UNITED STATES OF AMERICA BY
UNITED PRINTING SERVICES, INC.
NEW HAVEN, CONN.

For
Elisabeth

Preface

FREDERICK GODDARD TUCKERMAN'S sonnets, written to satisfy a private need, form a personal journal of a poet who sought to bring into order a life assailed by doubt and grief on one hand and fortified by certitude of its worth on the other. The sonnets draw their strength from a deeply subjective series of experiences; the first person singular always refers to Tuckerman, and it never attains a wider scope or a greater identity. His intention was to record as objectively as possible the struggle between a mind tormented by personal tragedy and a spirit sustained by hope. The conquest by the spiritual force signaled a triumph of tremendous proportions when viewed in the light of the opposing elements. The sonnets move inexorably from despair to tragedy to an unmistakable optimism. Tuckerman's aim was always clear, and the extent of his success may be judged by the sympathetic reader. He asserted that he had written the sonnets only for those who could understand and in this way established their autobiographical nature.

Without a message for all mankind, without the slightest tincture of the universal, the sonnets failed to gain recognition among New Englanders grown accustomed to poetry which masked or completely hid the purely personal. But when newer generations accepted intimate revelation as a staple of poetry, Tuckerman was able to assume an increasingly important place among his more famous and illustrious contemporaries.

The best of his poetry, in circulation for more than thirty years, is still not widely known. Within recent years, however, evidence has been collecting to insure its eventual recognition and appreciation. The fame and approval which he mildly sought but finally abandoned are beginning to come; those who have encountered his sonnets have been pleased to note their general excellence and wonder why they have been so slow in making their way. What little critical comment has been written has been uniformly favorable. Walter Prichard Eaton, Witter Bynner, the New York critics in the 1930's, Yvor Winters, Mordecai Marcus, Stanley T. Williams, Edmund Wilson, and

N. Scott Momaday have registered warm approval and in each instance, after making allowances for some poetic nodding, have agreed that Tuckerman is much too good a poet to be allowed to remain in obscurity. It seems high time that his life and his work be given a fuller hearing and exposure to hasten his poetic prosperity.

In writing about a poet so rarely read and so seldom noticed, it is easy to persuade oneself to assume the role of a vigorous apologist, lavishing high praise on the subject and chiding his dispraisers. In this study I have tried to avoid this temptation; the presentation seeks to allow Tuckerman to be seen modestly so that he, himself, may have the opportunity to display his poetry and to allow it to speak for itself.

His biography and his work are inseparable. A knowledge of his life invigorates the sonnets and enhances understanding of their meaning and purpose. I have divided his biography into two parts: one, a collection of the facts of his life to form an outer biography; the other, a view of his character, thoughts, and personality to account for his inner biography. Against the placid background of the first, there stands in sharp relief the image of a complicated, vexed spirit. Since spiritual autobiography must be an intimate thing, I have thought it expedient to let the poet tell his own story and to have the last word without a critical intermediary.

After dealing with the vagaries of his poetical fortunes in his day and in our own, I have undertaken to examine his sonnets so that their autobiographical aspects will help remove possible auras of obscurity and vagueness and thereby leave a clear view of an elegant and candid recorder of the experiences of one who was able to objectify his inner life. In addition, I have tried to reveal some of the technical devices in his sonnets and to point to his magnificent use of New England's nature without labeling him a "naturalist-poet."

Aside from the sonnets, his only important work is *The Cricket*, which is given a chapter to itself. My presentation of its worth and its meaning is conditioned, and perhaps prejudiced, by the premise that it is an extension of the underlying thoughts and feelings expressed in the sonnet series. The remainder of his work contains some nuggets worth saving. This salvage is necessary for a fuller grasp of the scope and potentiality of his power.

Frugality is a hallmark of Yankee tradition. Its poetry is rich but never so rich that it can be profligate enough to ignore or to discard any of its poetic gold. Here is a small but rare treasure to be added to the hoard of New England poets who so lately have been given the sovereign stamp. It is good to know Tuckerman and it is satisfying to lengthen the list of New England poets by placing his name alongside those of Edward Taylor, Emily Dickinson, and Jones Very.

The debts I gratefully acknowledge are few but heavy: Mr. Orton Loring Clark of Amherst, Massachusetts, for his generosity in providing me with access to the Tuckerman Papers when they were in his possession; the staff of the Houghton Library at Harvard University for continued access when they were removed there; the keepers of the books in the Boston Athenaeum and of the public records in Greenfield, Massachusetts; and, Wayne State University for a Faculty Research Fellowship for time in which to prepare the material.

SAMUEL A. GOLDEN

Wayne State University

Contents

Chronology

1821 Frederick Goddard Tuckerman born in Boston, Massachusetts.

1833 Attends Bishop Hopkins's School in Burlington, Vermont.

1837 Enters Harvard College.

1838 Quits Harvard College.

1839 Re-enters Harvard in The Law School.

1842 Graduates from law school.

1844 Admitted to Suffolk (County) Bar in Massachusetts.

1847 Marries Hannah Lucinda Jones of Greenfield, Massachusetts.

1847 Leaves Boston to settle in Greenfield.

1850 Poetry begins to appear in print. "May flowers," *Littell's Living Age,* October 19.

1851 First trip abroad.

1854 Second trip abroad—meeting with Tennyson—start of long friendship.

1857 Death of his wife.

1860 Private printing of *Poems.*

1863 British edition of *Poems.*

1864 First American edition of *Poems.*

1867 Plans to leave Greenfield—correspondence with Mrs. Nathaniel Hawthorne about buying Wayside in Concord.

1869- Second American edition of *Poems*—death of his son,
1871 Edward—gives up plan to move to Concord.

1873 Dies in Greenfield, Massachusetts—buried in Federal Street Cemetery.

Chronology

CHAPTER *1*

Biography: 'As the years unfold'

I *The Intellectual Milieu*

"Nor born to fame beneath some rare
Conspiracy of stars"

ONCE LITERATURE in the United States had achieved the
status of an authentic American literature, the direction it
was to take was never in question. The Romantic spirit was abroad
in the land and it found fertile fields for growth. Expression of
the spirit grew out of national expansion on the plains, in the
burgeoning cities, and along the seaboard. Industry, farming, and
commerce fostered self-reliance, originality, and enterprise. Under such conditions, exaltation of the limitless horizon and high
promise of success ingrained themselves not only in the pioneer
but even in the poor and downtrodden, memorialized in Emma
Lazarus's famous sonnet.

What Ralph Waldo Emerson had to say from the rostrum of
the lyceum and what he wrote in his books and in his essays
articulated brilliantly the Romantic ideas already firmly rooted
in the country. However, no established school of poets bound
strictly to a codified *modus operandi* came out of his teachings.
Nothing developed in America resembling the poetic phalanx in
the Dryden and Pope tradition, nor in the poetic affinity in style
and diction in Wordsworth, Shelley, and Keats. For better or for
worse, American poetry, like its creators, maintained and asserted
the efficacy of the ideas of independence and of reliance upon
the Self. Essentially the thinking tended to be the same in large
matters, but in manner of expression and in attitude lay the
crucial difference. One good illustration of this similarity and
diversity may be noted by comparing Henry Wadsworth Long-

fellow and Walt Whitman on the subject of universality in literature. In *Kavanagh,* Longfellow's schoolteacher, Mr. Churchill, says:

> Nationality is a good thing to a certain extent, but universality is better. All that is best in the great poets of all countries is not what is national in them, but what is universal. Their roots are in their native soil; but their branches wave in the unpatriotic air, that speaks the same language unto all men, and their leaves shine with the illimitable light that pervades all lands. Let us throw all the windows open; let us admit the light and air on all sides; that we may look toward the four corners of the heavens, and not always in the same direction.

In *Democratic Vistas,* Whitman apostrophizes Christ, the Greeks, Dante, and Shakespeare:

> Ye powerful and resplendent ones! ye were, in your atmospheres, grown not for America, but rather for her foes, the feudal and the old—while our genius is democratic and modern. Yet could ye, indeed, but breathe your breath of life into our New World's nostrils—not to enslave us, as now, but, for our needs, to breed a spirit like your own—perhaps (dare we to say it?) to dominate, even destroy, what you yourselves have left! On your plane, and no less, but even higher and wider, must we mete and measure for today and here. I demand races of orbic bards, with unconditional, uncompromising sway. Come forth, sweet democratic despots of the west!

It is important to note that ideas rampant in the mid-nineteenth century were common property; what is surprising to note is the suddenness with which the independence made itself felt and how divergent became the individual poetic utterance. Even to the cursory reader each important poet had an unmistakable voice and wrote in his own idiom—both as distinctive as his signature. It is, for example, impossible to fail to identify Whitman's "barbaric yawpings," or not to recognize Emily Dickinson's plaintive whisperings. On the other hand, among the older generation of poets, it would be relatively easy to confuse the voices of William Cullen Bryant and Longfellow.

Along with the diversity of voices, there developed, inevitably, a diversity of types of poetry; almost every form had its champion. The narrative of Longfellow, the confessional of Dickinson, the mystical revelation of Whitman, the economical

stanzas of Emerson, the sonnets of Frederick Goddard Tuckerman—all are representative of the wide variety of types. Least
popular in the 1860's was the sonnet. Its form and order and
its apparent relationship with the British sonnet put it, perhaps,
a little out of step with current American Romanticism and
nationalism. Somehow, the form did not fit into the untamed
spirit and the rugged contour of the land; it smacked of refine-
ment, sophistication, and urbanity. Even the excellent sonnets
of Longfellow never challenged the popularity of his narratives
and homilies. The time was not ripe for appreciation of the sonnet form and those who chose to use it had to face up to the
reality of neglect or, at best, to reluctant recognition. How low
in esteem the sonnet was held may be noted in a glance through
anthologies. For example, Perry Miller's *The Golden Age of
American Literature* includes only one sonnet, Poe's "To Science"; and Norman Foerster's section on the Romantic movement in *American Poetry and Prose* contains the same sonnet by
Poe and eleven by Longfellow. These examples, easily multiplied, show the lack of public acceptance of the sonnet at that
time.

After the nation had survived its ordeal of civil war and had
developed a more cosmopolitan, urban manner and tone, the
sonnet form was able to win an important niche in American
literature. The movement of the sonnet as a germane, native
form had started in the second half of the nineteenth century,
had gone underground, and then emerged in the twentieth
century. The sonnet was admirably adapted to mirror the
newer ways of the country and was most suitable for exploita-
tion of personal expression. The first great period of this form
in America came, therefore, in the early decades of the twentieth
century. Its roster is graced by such fine poets as Edwin
Arlington Robinson, William Ellery Leonard, and Edna St.
Vincent Millay; but by no stretching could the roster be made
to accommodate the older sonneteers: Longfellow, Jones Very,
and Frederick Goddard Tuckerman.

While reasons for Tuckerman's failure to win sustained support are considered throughout this volume, it needs to be
emphasized that his misfortune had been to write in an untimely genre. But, it is his ultimate good fortune that, with the
passing of time, the very characteristics which condemned him
to oblivion in his day were those which gave him a reprieve

and a new place in American literature. Popularity is a transient thing; literary reputations often run in crazy patterns in the writing and in the rewriting of literary history. But for Tuckerman, there was never any doubt that his contemporaries would be content to pass him by; for his final reputation—once the full scope of his work became known—there was no doubt either.

It has taken almost a century for the poetry of Frederick Goddard Tuckerman to gain a permanent place in the history of American literature. His contemporaries were drawn to his conventional lyrics and narratives, and they registered their interest politely and mildly. The next generation was silent; but, when twentieth-century readers rediscovered his work, they were attracted to the sonnets and found in them ample merit to warrant his inclusion among the better poets of New England. They recognized the worth of his successful experimentation with form and language, and they heard a new voice speaking out of the rural regions of western Massachusetts.

The single volume published during Tuckerman's lifetime, *Poems*, made a timid entrance into the poetic world. Privately printed in 1860, it was designed not to gain a wide audience but to solicit the reactions of his friends and the appraisal of established writers and critics. When Tuckerman sent presentation copies, he asked the recipients for their comments. Emerson, Longfellow, Bryant, Hawthorne, Jones Very, George S. Hillard, T. W. Parsons, George Ripley, and Henry T. Tuckerman responded dutifully, sympathetically, and, at times, brilliantly.[1] Such private circulation and commentary did very little to advance his popular reputation, but there were slight subsidiary benefits. For example, Emerson praised "Rhotruda" and eventually included it in his own anthology, *Parnassus*.[2] A London edition of *Poems* appeared in 1863 and a Boston one in 1864; both were rather favorably reviewed. The second Boston edition in 1869 was scarcely noticed. Tuckerman and his lone volume passed so quickly into oblivion that, by the time of his death in 1873, both he and his work were completely forgotten.

In 1909 Walter Prichard Eaton read a few of the sonnets, saw their excellence, and wrote a laudatory essay which gave a strong impetus to the complete recovery of Tuckerman as a poet.[3] To Eaton, it did not "seem just or right" that this poet was "so absolutely unknown in the history of American letters." The essay stirred members of the Tuckerman family to renew their own interest. The poet's daughter-in-law, Mrs. Frederick Tuckerman and his granddaughter, Mrs. Orton Loring Clark, along with Witter Bynner, searched through the poet's papers and unearthed three posthumous sonnet sequences. They added these to the two sequences which were part of the printed volume and in 1931 brought out an edition of the five sonnet sequences.[4] For the first time, a fuller extent of Tuckerman's best work became known. Bynner's perceptive preface and the appreciative reviews of his edition established Tuckerman as a poet worthy of a full hearing and of a place alongside many of his famous New England contemporaries. The appreciation and recognition now began in earnest.

In *Oxford Anthology of American Literature*, (1938), William Rose Benét and Norman Holmes Pearson, who reprinted six sonnets from the Bynner edition, justified their choice with the belief that the sonnets "seem to have been written ahead of their time" and that what bad poets had "customarily rendered silken and sleek he dared to give homeliness and rough strength."[5] In 1939 Walter E. Prince told an audience at Amherst College that "just as Walt Whitman and Emily Dickinson were neglected by their contemporaries, so Tuckerman failed to win recognition that he deserved."[6] The next year, Van Wyck Brooks observed that the sonnets were "admirable in craftsmanship, firm, fresh and clear . . . [and] were memorable expressions of tragic feeling."[7] In 1948 Louis Untermeyer printed six sonnets in *An Anthology of the New England Poets from Colonial Times to the Present* and in 1950 George F. Whicher included all twenty-eight sonnets of the first sequence in his anthology, *Poetry of the New England Renaissance. The Cricket,* another posthumous work, first published in 1950, was eloquently described by Yvor Winters as "one of the great meditations on death to be written since the seventeenth century" and as "probably the greatest single American poem of the nineteenth century. . . ."[8]

My monograph *Frederick Goddard Tuckerman: An American Sonneteer* (1952) contained a biography and a general survey of the poetry, and my article "Frederick Goddard Tuckerman: A Neglected Poet" (1956) in *The New England Quarterly* was an effort to push back the obscurity that still surrounded the poet. In 1960 *The Cricket* was printed in *The Massachusetts Review* with a preface by Mordecai Marcus, who said that this reprinting was "a service to lovers of poetry and students of American literature."[9] He followed this appreciation with a study of selected sonnets in *Discourse*.[10] In 1962 Edmund Wilson digressed long enough in *Patriotic Gore* to salute Tuckerman; and, while regretting that this poet "is still not well-known today," Wilson was moved to announce that he "has emerged at last from the obscurity which the retirement of his life invited."[11] Tuckerman's stature was further increased in 1963 when Warren Taylor included four sonnets in *Poetry in English,* an anthology containing some of the most distinguished poetry in English over the past six hundred years. In 1965 N. Scott Momaday edited *The Complete Poems of Frederick Goddard Tuckerman.* In his introduction he says, "Tuckerman's poems are valuable in their own right. They are the best possessions of a man whose vision is keen and whose judgment is sound."[12]

From this charting of his poetic fortunes, it is possible to state that Tuckerman is very likely to be rid at last of the adjectives "forgotten" and "neglected." New interest is destined to follow the basically sound pattern set by Bynner, who wrote that this New Englander "is as modern as any twentieth century sonneteer" and who referred, of course, to the better poets of the 1920's.[13] Such indications have already been set by Stanley T. Williams, who believed that Tuckerman "exhibited [a] restless search for a new technique" and that, like Lanier and Dickinson, he was one of the heralds of the great changes impending in the poetry of America[14] and by Edmund Wilson, who noted his modernity in the invention of words, "very much in the manner of Joyce."[15] But Tuckerman never thought of himself as a pioneer; he went his solitary way exploiting the sonnet form, experimenting with diction and imagery to satisfy only himself. As he once told Hawthorne, his work was "not written to please anybody, and is addressed to those only who understand it."

A Brahmin, a Transcendentalist, and a Romantic, Tuckerman early came under the powerful influences of Emerson, Wordsworth, and Tennyson; but, when he matured and grew strong enough to free himself from these influences, he emerged as a poet intent on listening to the beat of his own heart and on seeing his world through his own eyes. "Shall I," he asked,

> Who yield slow reverence where I cannot see
> And gather gleams where'er by chance or choice
> My footsteps draw, though brokenly dispensed—
> Come into light at last?[16]

His life story is the answer to that query.

II *His Background and his Youth*

"Those fair days"

The Tuckermans came from England to Massachusetts about 1649 and quickly established themselves as a prosperous and illustrious family during the first flush of Boston's growth. The poet's father, Edward Tuckerman, who was less famous than his brother, Joseph, the preacher and philanthropist, engaged in business and became a rich merchant. In association with such influential Bostonians as William Phillips, John Lowell, Josiah Quincy, William E. Channing, and Elisha Ticknor, he helped transform the city from a seaport into a metropolis which could boast of The Massachusetts General Hospital, The Boston Dispensary, The Massachusetts Bible Society, and The Boston Athenaeum, as well as of the first savings bank north of Philadelphia. Along with his mercantile, civic, cultural, and philanthropic interests, Edward was actively concerned with religious matters. His grandparents and his parents had been closely identified with the Episcopal Church; but, when he was twenty-one, he joined the Unitarian Church, first as a member of the Hollis Street Church, later as a member of the parish of William E. Channing and then that of Francis Parkman. However, in 1813 Edward had a change of heart and rejoined the Episcopal Church as a member of St. Paul's, where he eventually became a proprietor, a vestryman, a member of the standing committee of the Diocese, and a trustee of the Massachusetts Episcopal Theological School.[17]

Successful in business, Edward gave his children opportunities and freedom to devote their lives to pursuits congenial to their own interests and talents; at the same time, however, he exerted considerable control and influence over their religious training and education. He wanted to be sure that they would be free from what his son, the poet, was to call "the vexed conditions of his [own] heritage."[18] Thus, Edward, his eldest son, was sent to Union College rather than to Harvard because of possible contamination by the spiritual forces then rampant in Cambridge. Later the father relented and allowed Edward to spend many years at Harvard studying botany, literature, and religion.[19] Samuel Parkman, the second son, was organist and director of the choir at St. Paul's in Boston and succeeded Dr. Edward Hodges as organist in Trinity Church, New York. In addition, he published two collections of hymn tunes and anthems, and lectured extensively on cathedral music.[20] Frederick Goddard, the third son, also felt the strong impact of his father's concern; he was sent to Burlington to be educated in the school run by Bishop John Henry Hopkins, first Protestant Episcopal Bishop in Vermont. Sophia May, the youngest child, less supervised than her three brothers in religious upbringing, married David Eckley, a clergyman, son of the eminent Dr. Joseph Eckley, minister of the Old South Church from 1779 to 1811.[21]

Such parental preoccupation left an indelible mark on the poet's memory. He solemnly recalled: "O Father, God, to whom in happier days/My father bade me cry when troubles fall."[22] And he could reminisce about his youth when his own father was a close rival to God, the Father. In Sonnet V, Part III, he remembers running homeward across Boston Common during a thunder shower and hearing "God's anger mutter in the darkened heaven," but the scope of the sonnet is so sharply limited that the divine muttering seems to come not so much from heaven as from a room in the big family house at 33 Beacon Street.[23]

The factual biography of the youth and early manhood of Frederick Goddard Tuckerman reads like an exemplar of the rearing and education traditional among rich, well-connected Bostonians. Born in Boston on February 4, 1821, he was named for a kinsman who had traveled in Switzerland with Wordsworth, and whose accidental drowning was the subject of Wordsworth's "Lines upon a Young American Mr. F. W. Goddard, who was drowned in the Lake of Zurich."[24] True to the Brahmin tradition, his parents ingrained in him correctness of manners, respect for others, and impeccable decorum. Two scraps of juvenilia attest to this training. One is a note from an "affectionate cousin" who admonished him, "I think you try to be good . . . but you must be gentle and patient and mind quick." The other, which sounds like a penitent's earnest resolution to reform, he wrote when only ten years old. On the morning of August 15, 1831, he promised ". . . to try to behave better at table and to try to break myself of being so set and always wanting to have just what I like best all the time. This rule must be strictly observed by F. G. Tuckerman."

His early schooling matched his domestic training. In the same week that he had written this boyish resolve he participated in an exercise in declamation at the anniversary exhibition of Chauncy-Hall School in Boston, reciting the role of Orozimbo in a scene from Kotzebue's *Pizarro*. It is hard to imagine a Boston boy of ten acting as an old Peruvian hero, but it is easy to see the influence of such an experience. The poet recaptures the brave Orozimbo's bombastic defiance of brutal Pizarro when he revives

> . . . those fair days, when glorying
> I stood a boy amid the mullein-stalks
> And dreamed myself like him the Lion-King.
> There, where his shield shed arrows and the clank
> Clashed on his helm of battle-axe and brand,
> He pushed the battle backward, rank on rank
> Fallen in the sword-swing of his stormy hand.[25]

Neither Orozimbo nor Pizarro were Lion-Kings, but their fulsome rhetoric in this heroic tragedy with its fuss, fury, and noise are well trapped in these lines of adolescent imagination.

In 1833 Frederick was released from the personal control of his parents to continue at Bishop Hopkins's School in Burlington, Vermont. There he studied Latin, music, drawing, gardening—all, no doubt, interlaced with solid Episcopal homiletics. In a note to his brother, Edward, he wrote that the Bishop had divided the boys into companies with leaders and commanders. "The Bishop has two motives for doing so," he observed. "One is it teaches us to be obedient to our elders who, are generally much wiser and better than we are and it also teaches the leader, it is his duty to give good advice and prevent if possible those who he sees doing wrong."

Although the tightly-knit, disciplined Brahmin fraternity endorsed and encouraged conformity to its own notions of gentility and good breeding, inherent restlessness for independence, expressions of individuality, and strength of character very often resulted in rebellion. The obstinate and enduring streak of independence had not been eradicated from the Tuckerman family. The poet's father had broken with the Episcopal Church in defiance of his parents, and Joseph Tuckerman, an uncle, was always outspoken and prone to differ sharply with William E. Channing, his fellow-Unitarian. Therefore, it is neither surprising nor strange to see the next generation exhibiting its inheritance. Outwardly, young Tuckerman endured the regimen and rigors of Bishop Hopkins's classroom, but he constantly yearned to run into the woods and fields where he could shed discipline and blind obedience and avoid a world he neither understood nor valued. The poetry is replete with glimpses and snatches of his youthful, rebellious ways. In Sonnet XXIX, Part II, he confesses that, "with some pretext of o'erwrought sight" and "dazzled with decimal and dividend," he went running forth "to Nature as to a friend!" He boasts of his self-learning because from it he

> Knew each bleached alder-root that plashed across
> The bubbling brook and every mass of moss;
> Could tell the month, too, by the vervain-spike,—
> How far the ring of purple tiny flowers
> Had climbed—just starting, maybe, with the May,
> Half-high, or tapering off at summer's end.

In Sonnet IV, Part III, he feels "assuaged and soothed/And happier made," by bringing to mind carefree after-school times when, with companions, he ". . . hunted on, from flower to frosty flower,/Tattered and dim the last red butterfly,/Or the old grasshopper molasses-mouthed." His insatiate desire to wander from familiar paths is at the very heart of Sonnet V, Part III. He knew that God's anger would fall on him if he entered "through the forbidden gate," the old "burial place that at the corner stood." Yet he went there knowing well the high price he would have to pay.

The happiest days of his youth were the rebellious ones. Strong-willed and stubborn, he knew exactly where he was most happy and meant to linger and loiter there. In a state of "innocent grace," he wandered about to discover the glory of ". . . the early bee/On the maple log, the white-heaped cherry tree/That hummed all day in the sun, the April blue."[26] He was most at home in the fields and woods because he felt there that his quick insight into the workings of nature was almost divine. But these wonderful days of boyhood so liberally spread across the pages of his poetry were tempered by a vague, disturbing sense of something deeper in nature than simple observation and innocent sport. Feelings of exhilaration fused with those of disquieting mystery often disturbed and marred his enchantment. Recollecting holidays spent in Canada and on Long Island, he confesses that

> . . . even mid merry boyhood's tricks and scapes,
> Early my heart a deeper lesson learnt,—
> . . . .
> And I have stood, beneath Canadian sky,
> In utter solitudes where the cricket's cry
> Appals the heart and fear takes visible shapes,
> And on Long Island's void and isolate capes
> Heard the sea break like iron bars.[27]

Long Island was a favorite vacation place where he enjoyed listening to local lore. Once he had heard a tale "craftily quaint" and was pleased with the romance he had felt in "the secret seed/Of song or story marvelous" and added that "Here did my dreaming childhood, listening, brood/On tales of wind and shipwreck." In this way the sternness of Long Island's "void and isolate capes" was softened.

The serenity of Frederick's youthful days was further clouded by the thought of the inevitability of the passage of youth. In "As Sometimes In a Grove" he records the disturbing regret that, once he had "seen his morning go,/Nor dreamed it mattered," "Must he then, fail, because his youth went wide?"[28] In later life he would mourn for those irretrievable days, knowing that, "in a world with joy and sorrow torn," "No life is sweeter/Than his, just starting in his journey's morn."[29]

Tuckerman's love of nature and his feeling of a mystic union with it did not mean that he was in open rebellion against the strictures of formal education. When he returned to Boston, he was enrolled first in The Boston Latin School; then, at the age of sixteen, he entered Harvard College with the class of 1841. After one year he quit. T. W. Higginson, a classmate, remembered him as a "refined and gentlemanly fellow" but "not as a poet"; he guessed incorrectly that Tuckerman had left for the same reason his brother, Edward, had been sent to Union College.[30] This supposition is unsound because in 1837 Edward had been permitted to come to Harvard despite the possible dangers of overexposure to Unitarianism. The poet's son thought that "serious trouble with his eyes" was the real reason.[31] Whatever the reason, the following year Frederick returned, enrolled in the Harvard Law School, and took the degree of LL.B. in 1842. An inkling as to how he felt about the years at Harvard may be seen in this short statement he had written in a scrapbook: "Frederick G. Tuckerman came home to *live* in May 1843." Two years later he was admitted to the Suffolk (County) Bar in Massachusetts; worked part of a year in the Boston law office of Edward D. Sohier, an old family friend; and then abandoned the legal profession. This excursion into the study of law which seems so foreign to his youthful ways is in keeping with Yankee tradition. The Brahmin and New England way was practical and shrewd enough to insist that a man have a definite profession even if he had financial independence and wished to follow a life that promised more shadow than substance. T. W. Parsons was a dentist and a poet; George S. Hillard, a lawyer and a litterateur. Hawthorne, Emerson, Thoreau, and many other New Englanders had trades or professions to help support their literary careers.

Tuckerman's poetry is strangely silent about the years at Harvard. His lack of interest in the practice of law and his subsequent development as a poet make it quite safe to assume that he used those years for wide reading of English literature and for keeping abreast of current New England writing and thought. One bit of evidence supports this assumption: in 1844 he decided (so he told Joseph D. Story, the distinguished jurist, who had been his professor at the law school) to go abroad to "gratify his curiosity as well as to reinstate himself in health." Plans had advanced to the stage where Tuckerman asked Judge Story for a letter of introduction to Lord Morpeth who had been a visitor in the Tuckerman home. The letter said nothing about Tuckerman's legal skill but spoke "with the utmost sincerity of his talents, his character and his literary attainments." The whole project came to nothing and apparently Tuckerman was content to remain in New England. This mention of "his literary attainments" is the first notice anyone had made of his writing.

III   *A Poet in the Making*

" 'Twas hit or miss"

The college years over, he was at last free to make whatever he wished of his life. It is certain and not surprising that he found living on Beacon Hill unpleasant. For one of his independent temperament, the high society of Boston was irksome. He admitted that in the city his perception of beauty "had been dulled to sleep, by disappointment, doubt, and worldly wear" and that he was oppressed by "the fear of wrong, and coldness everywhere."[32] Many years later his sister Sophia would write to him from Florence, Italy, and in a rare, unguarded moment, wonder if the reason for their separation and removal from Boston had been due to the way "we were brought up, to hide our feelings, to be insincere, or was it the crushing atmosphere of the Boston influence."

At this stage in his life Tuckerman saw no urgency to rush into a career; instead, he enjoyed the freedom of a young gentleman of leisure, permitting time to pass pleasantly and even elegantly while he turned an idle phrase. A dreamer, yet a realist, he considered himself a trifler of time. This general impression is strengthened by a trio of very early works, "A Latter-Day Saint," "Anybody's Critic," and "A Sample of Coffee-Beans," which are chiefly of value as they help reconstruct the biography of the poet in the making.

In "A Latter-Day Saint" he tried his hand at verbal portraiture, but the verses turn away from the subject and call attention to his evident delight in tinkering with Hudibrastic rhymes. He does not wish to be taken seriously; he prefers to draw a smile at his callow ingenuity. For example, he rhymes "beard" with "heard," "Jerusalem" with "himself and them." The latter-day saint ". . . stood, and saw the great world fume and foam on,/As on a dial-plate, himself the gnomon." And, at the end of the piece he ". . . smeared with mud and yellow yolks is,/ Giving the law, like Zeno or Zamolxis."

This sort of pseudo-cleverness is carried over into "Anybody's Critic" as he rhymes "rebuke" with "look" and outrageously couples "uplands grassy" with "Burgelostrassé." But the true emphasis is on his polite and mildly satiric attitude toward the ignorant critic, a descendant of Dick Minim:

> . . . But view our Critic! mark his eye
> Exhaustive, nose would snuff the violet dry
> Of odour, and a brow to whelm the world.

"A Sample of Coffee-Beans" is a more ambitious effort. The simple narrative of how Tuckerman was duped by a Yankee pedlar at a village inn in northern New Hampshire into buying fake coffee-beans becomes the over-elaborate frame for his own portrait.[33] In a jovial mood, he tells the story in blatantly mock-heroic lines. For example,

> The bean, the garden-bean, I sing,—
> Lima, mazagan, late and early,
> Bush, butter, blackeye, pole and string,
> Esculent, annual, planted yearly:

and,

> As Io fled by Nigris' stream,—
> Spurred by the angry brize or bot-bee:
> But beans I sing, a classic theme
> Known to the Muse: . . .

The self-portrait is the only real asset of this piece. Tuckerman has drawn himself so vividly and so accurately that, in the light of his future development, he has taken a precise measure of his character, his temperament, and his interests. He looks at himself from four angles. In the first, he is "a poet slim" leaving the village to go to the inn; but, even as he approaches it, he realizes that "In the world-drama he was one,/Bearing, perhaps, a part like Peto/In the old play."[34] At the same time, unlike Peto, he shunned

> The world, and, reckless of mosquito,
> By pond-hole dark, and weedy drain,
> Sequestered swamp, or grassy side-hill,
> Would linger, breathing dull disdain
> In many a rustic ode and idyll.

The second view is that of a neophyte laboring to produce good verses. The sharp focus is on his own ineptitude. Laughing at his efforts, he turns the laughter into self-satire as he mockingly brags that his verses brim with beauty, wit, and poetic ardor. The persiflage continues as he likens himself to Shakespeare by bringing attention to some famous lines of Ben Jonson that contain the image of the poet hammering hard to shape clumsy lines but inexpertly hitting the anvil twice and only once "upon the burning iron." Tuckerman pompously confesses that, while his work is hit or miss, he is "not quite a Walter Scott or Byron."

The third picture concentrates on an appraisal of his character. The paradox of avoiding people yet wanting to be near them is developed here. He says that "Good fellow was he in the main,/Yet strangely strove to be unhappy." He strongly suggests that he has an uncontrollable imagination. Sometimes he thinks of himself as a desert-chief and at others as a lonely wanderer weeping "to cleanse/Some fancied shame or felony." But balanced against this observation is a much more complete picture of himself at ease in his chamber where he lies, bemused by an old tale, or where he lingers among his "blotted sheets, and rolls o'erwritten" and is happy "to read and rant his rhymes,/Unwearied with their repetition."[35]

In the fourth view, he knows he has not yet mastered the poet's craft but is confident and proud of his mastery of botany and astronomy. With candor he says that

> Full well he knew the stars and flowers,
> The atmosphere, its height and pressure,
> The laws that gird the globe, and powers
> That make our peril or our pleasure.

The portraits of the yolk-smeared fanatic, of the false critic, and of the fledgling poetaster are mere flirtations with the Muse. But Tuckerman quickly abandoned this sort of trifling and began to grow into a serious poet. Maturity came rapidly, and the reason behind this swift change from a poetic idler is his courtship of Hannah Lucinda Jones of Greenfield in western Massachusetts. The change of attitude appears in two poems telling of his love. "Elidore" might be hastily overlooked as just one more example of a Tennysonian girl-name piece; but, when the deceptive title is explicated, there is no doubt that Tuckerman is talking directly about his love for Hannah Lucinda. Elidore, an invention, is either a variant of Eleanore or a compounded name made up from Eleanore and Dorothy. Eleanore means "light" as does Lucinda; Dorothy, "gift of God";

and Ann, or Hannah, Grace, a gift of God. Thus, in selecting "Elidore" for the title, he is indulging in slight disguise. The poem itself, which abounds with references to grace and light, removes any doubt as to its true subject.

His meeting with Hannah, he says, is a welcome relief from the "tricks of female guile" he had previously encountered. Rejoicing in her "childlike grace and plain sincerity," he envisions her "a wonder of the earth" with

> A graceful mind, most gracefully inclosed;
> A woman fair and young, but softly free
> From the world's wisdom, and hypocrisy;
> Or restless spite, or curiosity;
> Gentle and glad, yet armed in constancy,
> With breathings heavenward, and a faith composed.

Through her grace and beauty all darkness dissolved, and a new joy "relumed his vision dim." He feels like a "wood-lost wanderer" who "discerns a peering light,/And sees it shine, a star of safety." Grace and Light (Hannah and Lucinda) merge "as that strange beauty beamed/To illume a heart, that had its grace, its power, misdeemed."

"The Question," a much more luxuriantly conceived poem and the first one to reveal Tuckerman's promising power as a poet, is filled with great joy. It is a riot of sound and color. He asks the simple question, "How shall I array my fair?" After considering many possibilities, he thinks in terms of

> Pearl, and priceless marbles bright,—
> Onyx, myrrhine, marcasite,
> And jasper green!—

For an alternative, he suggests bedecking her preciously with

> Jewels crossed with jewels gleam
> On jewels, jewel-circled there;
> While, round her wrists and ankles bare,
> Gems of jewels glimpse and gaze,—
> Hyacinth, rose-stone, idocrase.

Then he fancies her among "Shower myrtles, myrrh, and gum,/With heliochryse and ámomum!"

But all this Whitmanesque and epic cataloguing is discarded in favor of a much more direct and sensible answer. He is sure that her matchless beauty cannot be enhanced by exotic elements in nature, and that it is far more appropriate to let her beauty stand alone, "Lovely in the meadow-land,/With a clover in her hand." Years later, when he sent his copy to the press, he charged the printer to be very careful to print "clover," not "cleaver."

IV *The Maturing Poet*

"Why hold ye so my heart?"

Married in 1847, the Tuckermans moved to Greenfield and settled in a house on Church Street.[36] Even now Frederick was not fully certain of his career because the marriage record lists his occupation as lawyer, but he did not engage in legal work but became totally engrossed in botany, astronomy, meteorology, and poetry. Moreover, once free from Beacon Hill and Boston society, he never returned permanently to the opulent surroundings of his boyhood. Except for occasional trips to the Observatory in Cambridge and two extended visits to Europe, he spent the rest of his life in the Greenfield region. To satisfy his scientific interests in astronomy, he bought a fine telescope and for a few years kept an astronomical and meteorological journal.[37] The flora of Hancock County were so rich and varied that they afforded him ample opportunities for careful observation, and he was eventually recognized as an authority of the flora and fauna of the region. Surrounded now by such natural wealth, he drew upon it liberally in his serious writing of poetry.

The astronomical and meteorological journal, kept with fair regularity from October, 1847, to December 31, 1850, provides information to account for his activities during the early years in Greenfield; but, more importantly, it reveals the intensity of his interest in astronomy and botany which were to play such prominent roles in his poetry. Most of the entries are in the cryptic notations of the scientist, but occasionally there is an entry tinged with the poetic. For example, on April 7, 1848, between three and four o'clock in the morning, he observed the aurora. It appeared, he noted, "a solid arch of white light, crossing the meridian, a little north of the zenith; and the constellation of the Bear, hanging in the crimson glow of its outskirts, brought to mind, the 'Iamque rubescebat stellis *Aurora* fugates,' of Virgil; no crepitation however could be distinguished, though the air was clear and still, and the radiations uncommonly active and intense." During a nocturnal watch on May 27, 1848, he observed the waning moon; he called it a rare chance with "the atmosphere being perfectly tranquil and pellucid."

In his commonplace book he copied these lines from a poem in a newspaper:

(line 4) A full-orbed moon that, like thine own soul soaring,
(line 5) Sought a precipitant pathway up through heaven.

and observed that "If it was a "full-orbed moon" and *midnight* it *couldn't* have soared: The fifth line is incorrect as the moon must have been *on* the meridian at that time." Forty years[38] later he came across this notation and added a mellow note:

On perusing the foregoing forty years afterwards.
The objection is trivial and hypercritical as any object hanging in the sky may be poetically said to soar: The fifth line however is inexact.
Apology for the Foregoing.
The writer begs leave to withdraw his offensive expressions respecting the moon as totally uncalled for.
Afterthought.
Besides the moon was an enchanted moon.

Very often he would account for lacunae in his journal by noting that he was away from Greenfield. On January 15, 1848, he went to the Observatory at Cambridge to view "trapezium Orionis" (one of his favorite constellations), to examine drawings of the Nebulae Mars and to look at Sir F. W. Herschel's new work. In this journal he also kept an account of his discoveries of flowers emerging from the long winters. This sort of activity was of special concern, for he felt that nature had endowed him with a divine sense when, "by guarded insight fine," he saw "Cold April flowers in the green end of June."[39] His notations during 1849 show that on April 11 he found the first mayflowers on Prospect Hill; on April 25, anemones; and, two days later, the early dandelions appeared. On May 3, the first cowslips, blue violets, and adders [*sic*] tongue appeared. A week later, along the Connecticut River, he found the first columbine of the season. On May 11, by the banks of Green

River, he saw trillium, white and yellow violets, and, the next day, the first princes [*sic*] pine.

In addition to watching the skies and searching for early flowers, he climbed among the rocks near the summit of the western slope of Rocky Mountain where he had established a favorite haunt from which he could look down on the village and the rivers that bound it. The place became known as the Poet's Seat, a name still famous in Greenfield. A stone tower now marks the spot, but the visitor will find nothing there to memorialize the poet.

The stars and the flowers became the staple of Tuckerman's poetic life. From the very start of his literary career he felt so closely attached to them that they became sources of inspiration from which to extract elements to match exactly his personal moods. His earliest published work shows how quickly and surely he accomplished such correlation. "May flowers" appeared in the October 19, 1850, issue of *Littell's Living Age*. A pleasant bit of verse, it captures his preoccupation with the fashionable searching for spring flowers and also his delight in noting that children are made happy by the sight of mayflowers, a guarantee of nature's reawakening. He has seen alder spray and "willows gray," the cowslip and "the bloodroot's caps of silver"; but he preferred to bring back to the village trailing arbutus, the mayflower.

> Girlish heads, half-seen, and glancing,
> Peeped athrough the leaf-lorn bowers;
> And the little children, dancing,
> Clapped their hands, and cried, "May flowers!"

The same magazine in its issue of May 22, 1852, printed "Inspiration," "Infatuation," and the sonnet, "Again, again, ye part in stormy grief." In these poems the stars and the flowers also become the foundations for the expression of his feelings. In "Inspiration" the chief concern is with the stars as a guide; the poet, unable to find inspiration anywhere, turns in desperation to the stars. He confesses,

> I linger, watching for a warmer gleam,
> While still my spirit shivers, and I seem
> Like one constrained to wander
> Alone, till morning light,
> Beneath the hopeless grandeur
> Of a star-filled winter's night.

The sonnet, probably recalling the death of an infant daughter in 1848,[40] finds its base in the rain and wind that sweep across Greenfield in the fall and leave a scene of devastation to match his sorrow. Where once the spring flowers grew he sees "Pathetic Autumn, and the writhled leaf"; and, as he looks at the "wet black roofs," he brings the view into sharper focus to see "the raindrops strung along the blind."[41]

Still another early poem emphasizes Tuckerman's quick appreciation of the natural world which surrounded and even enveloped him. "Picomegan" appeared after considerable delay in *Putnam's Monthly Magazine* in July, 1854. The poem is crammed with the flora he has seen along the Picomegan (the Indian name for Green River) which flows past the boundary of Greenfield.[42] There is such profusion of flowers that he is overwhelmed. Along the river banks he finds "Stars of gold the green sod fretting," clematis, silvery moss, and alders. The river growths become exotic; he sees

> Bunches of the purple aster,
> Mints, and blood-dropped jewel-weed,
> Like carnelians hanging
> 'Mid their pale-green leaves.

Through such poems Tuckerman began to build a strange but real world. He endowed the Berkshire region with an elegance and wealth of natural resources not exceeded by the exciting place Thoreau made of Walden and Concord, by the microscopic private world that Emily Dickinson built in Amherst only a few miles from Tuckerman's Greenfield, or by the plaintive realm Bryant established in Cummington.

V   The First Trip Abroad

"The Pilgrim's steps"

His career barely launched, Tuckerman in the summer of 1851 made his first trip to Europe to visit those places closely associated with some of his favorite British poets. The record of his pilgrimage was carefully set down in a curious album entitled, "Wild Flowers gathered in Scotland and England during the Summer of 1851." In it he meticulously pressed botanical specimens and noted their names, the date, and the place where

he had gathered each one. For example, on May 14, he plucked
ground ivy at Gray's grave in Stokes; on July 2, jessamine at
Scott's cottage; and on July 5, mallows near Scott's grave at
Dryburgh Abbey. On July 9 he was at Grasmere, where he
picked some violet pansies at Wordsworth's cottage; on July 15,
at the churchyard in Stratford-on-Avon, he took some mallows.
When he visited Christ College gardens at Cambridge, July 23,
he took a sprig from Milton's mulberry as a memento. This
album is the sole record of the 1851 journey. Apparently he had
no contact with contemporary British poets at this time but
was satisfied to pay homage to the great poets—to gratify, at
last, the curiosity he had mentioned to Professor Story seven
years earlier.

Following this trip, Tuckerman returned to Greenfield.
Whereas his earlier work had been confined in the main to
verse within the tradition of Wordsworth and Tennyson, the
poetry he wrote after the trip underwent a decisive change.
By the time he made his second journey to England, he had
broken away from his highly derivative verse to write the first
of his sonnet sequences, which fulfilled the promise of excellence manifest in his conventional narratives and lyrics. During these years the Wordsworthian influence waned and that
of Tennyson grew with Tuckerman's development as a sonneteer. Once an admirer of Tennyson, whom he had given considerable space in a commonplace book to his poetry, he had changed
now from a mere admirer to a serious student. In the two
volumes of the London, 1842, edition of Tennyson's *Poems*,
acquired from his brother, Samuel Parkman, in 1850, Frederick
left unmistakable evidence of the new attitude.[43]

These particular volumes are especially valuable because
from them may be determined a great deal about Tuckerman's
readings in English poetry and the extent of his knowledge of
Tennyson's work. Both volumes contain abundant marginalia
to reveal how seriously Tuckerman had studied him. Most of
the notations are excerpts from other poets and call attention
to Tennyson's copious borrowings from them. They range freely
from Chaucer to Byron, from Shakespeare to Wordsworth, from
the Scriptures to Otway. Tuckerman notes, for example, that
"And did not dream it was a dream" in "The Two Voices" de-
rives from Shelley's "Absorbed like one within a dream who
dreams/That he is dreaming" and the line "Some yearning

toward the lamps of night" in the same poem echoes loudly Shakespeare's "He wastes the lamps of night." Or, in "The Day-Dream" Tennyson writes "Where on the double rosebud droops," and this phrase brings to mind Walter Scott's "lips like a double rosebud." "The Vision of Sin" is a pudding stone of borrowings from Wordsworth, Milton, Keats, Shelley, Chaucer, Shakespeare, Scott, and the Earl of Rochester. And, when he comes to the last line, "God made Himself an awful rose of dawn," Tuckerman comments, "The exact meaning or force of this line does not seem clear: Keats however has made use of the same image similarly—

> Hyperion, leaving twilight in the rear,
> Came slope upon the threshold of the west;
> Then, as was wont, his palace-door flew ope
>
> . . . .
>
> And like a rose in vermeil tint and shape,
>
> . . . .
>
> Stood full blown, for the God to enter in.
> (*Hyperion: A Fragment*)

Occasionally Tuckerman pounces on such a familiar epithet as "myriad-minded" in "Ode to Memory" and writes that it "is Coleridge's, applied (from the Greek) to Shakespeare." In many instances Tuckerman copied the original text in the margin to compare it with the altered version. For example, in "The Lady of Shalott" are these lines:

> And up and down the people go,
> Gazing where the lillies blow
> Round an island there below,
> The island of Shalott.

which were originally

> The yellow-leaved water lily,
> The green sheathed daffodilly
> Tremble in the water chilly
> Round about Shalott.

There are many more similar citations in "The Lady of Shalott," in "Mariana in the South," in "The Miller's Daughter," in "Oenone," and in several other poems. Another form of marginal note occurs in "Amphion." Here Tuckerman writes that "The very sparrows in the hedge" refers to Tennyson's brother poets, "A jackass heehaws from the rick" to the critic, and "The passive oxen gaping" to the public.

These notations are only a small sampling, but they are sufficient to make the point that Tuckerman was well versed in literature and profoundly immersed in Tennyson's poetry. Which of these notes were inscribed before Tuckerman's second visit to England is now impossible to ascertain, but there are several remarks which were obviously written after the Tennyson-Tuckerman meeting.

VI *The Second Trip Abroad: Tuckerman and Tennyson*

"In the 'wind-shaken attic'"

In the fall of 1854 Tuckerman returned to Europe and late in January, 1855, spent three or four memorable days with Tennyson at Farringford. He never forgot this visit and never tired of reminding his countrymen of it. While Tennyson disliked Americans in general, he was cordial to those who came to visit him on the Isle of Wight. As he had been to Emerson in 1848 and as he was later to Bayard Taylor and much later still to T. W. Higginson, so he was to Tuckerman. There is a story that Tennyson was cold to the young American because he thought him one of the horde of celebrity-seekers; but, after they had talked a while, Tennyson warmed to him: he realized that his visitor was very familiar with his work and could quote at length from it.[44] A remarkably close relationship now began. Even though Tuckerman was an unknown and virtually unpublished versifier, Tennyson chose to overlook this handicap and treated him with consideration and had respect for his literary judgment.

Tuckerman was fortunate in timing his visit to the mid-winter when Farringford was a lonesome place. They sat in Tennyson's attic and talked of many things. Tennyson said that he admired the works of Hawthorne and Poe and that he wanted to read more of them. He related the anecdote of his writing to Longfellow, a stranger, to request that he extend hospitality to Charles Weld, secretary of the Royal Society, who wished to make his acquaintance. Tennyson chanted several of his own poems and permitted the young American to comment on them.

After Tennyson had read "The Lotos Eaters," Tuckerman suggested the possibility that "strand" be substituted for "land" in the first line. Tennyson took the observation seriously. "In reading this Poem aloud," Tuckerman observed in the margins of his copy of Tennyson's *Poems*, "the author was quite struck by a suggestion, that he might have written 'strand' for 'land' in the first line."[45]

When Tennyson came to the lines "Is there confusion in the little isle?/Let what is broken so remain," he stopped to remark that "it was not usual for people to ask and answer their own questions."[46] Jokingly he told Tuckerman that the last line of "The Miller's Daughter," "I scarce should be unclasp'd at night," had been "objected to by lady critics as immodest."[47] He read "Mariana" and said that he considered it his best poem.[48] Then he read "The Idylls," "Maud," and some unpublished poems of which Tuckerman assured him he would "never repeat a word" until they were in print. When they discussed "The Charge of the Light Brigade," Tuckerman felt free to object to the rhyming of "blunder'd" with "Hundred," believing it should read "blundered." Tennyson remembered this comment and eventually made the change.

Unlike Emerson, who had had little opportunity to talk at length with Tennyson, Tuckerman had the pleasure of long and intimate conversations in front of the little fire in the "wind-shaken attic." The tone of their quick friendship was not that of an awestruck disciple at the feet of the master but of two poets chatting amiably and on occasion discussing poetry seriously. A relationship of equality and mutual respect, the warmth of the friendship may be measured in part by their exchange of gifts. When Tuckerman was ready to depart, his host presented him with the manuscript of "Locksley Hall" and in making the presentation said that "he never did such a thing in his life before, for anybody."[49] He also gave him two of his long, clay pipes; and Tuckerman subsequently reciprocated by sending a costly pipe, which Tennyson thought a poor exchange; the gift reminded him of old Glaucus in the *Iliad*, who had "exchanged his gold for the other's brass." However, the pipe served as a reminder of Tuckerman, for Tennyson wrote that it had "already acquired a mellow autumn brown which will no doubt deepen for many a long month as I sit and smoke to your memory." Another gift Tennyson accepted, perhaps tongue in cheek, was a Webster's dictionary bound in Russian leather. Later Tuckerman sent Tennyson the works of Poe and Hawthorne, and Tuckerman as late as 1861 told Hawthorne that he had just sent Tennyson a copy of the *Mosses*.

The visit was not limited to literary conversations. Tennyson took his guest into the family circle, and Lady Tennyson enjoyed having him in their home. Even young Hallam was aware of his presence. Tennyson wrote that "Little Hallam recollected you for three days as was to be gathered from his two expressions of Where's gemplum (gentleman) and Melliky (America). Then you faded and passed out of his horizon."

Back in Greenfield, Tuckerman apparently remembered every detail of the visit. What especially impressed him was Tennyson's manner of chanting his poems, and he used the Tennysonian chant whenever he recited his lines. He was so proud of this great episode in his life that he did not conceal his delight. One young friend called such a meeting "the event of a lifetime"; another hoped that Tuckerman would tell Tennyson how highly he was thought of in New England. Tuckerman was overjoyed to tell Hawthorne that he knew Tennyson and to repeat to Longfellow the anecdote about Mr. Weld. The news of Tuckerman's triumph spread to Concord for Emerson in a letter referred to "your friend Tennyson"; and in New York, as late as 1860, a reviewer reminded his readers that "Mr. Tuckerman is said to be a personal friend of Tennyson."[50]

The record of the meeting is preserved in their exchange of letters which began on January 31, 1855, and continued regularly through the better part of that year. The last extant correspondence is a portion of a letter from Tuckerman dated October 22, 1855, and Tennyson's reply to it. In it he defends Tennyson from the attacks on "Maud." "Only poets can fully appreciate and enjoy the singular beauty of 'Maud,'" he wrote. "The newspapers are loud, but the poet holds it to his heart in silence. I have seen the attack in *Blackwood*, and gather from it that the reviewer, whoever he may be, accords you the highest poetical rank, and his other propositions refute themselves, strange that people because they cannot appreciate or rightly understand a subject, abuse the treatment of it, which may be (and in this case is) wholly in keeping."[51]

Tuckerman goes on to admire "And clattering flints batter'd with clanging hoofs." He finds "Living alone in an empty house" a line unsurpassed "in literature of the kind, unless I except 'Mariana.' " "Go not happy day" he thinks a beautiful little song. He assured his correspondent that, "As for affecting your fame however or influencing the motions of the masses by a magazine article, a man might as well stand upon the sea-shore in a flood-tide and attempt to put the waves back with a pitch-fork." Tennyson thanked him for the critique and promised to send an early copy.

After this letter the only known correspondence is a note of consolation from Lady Tennyson to Mrs. Eckley, the poet's sister, upon his death in 1873: "No one, we know, can replace for you this life-long friend. I need not tell you that Mr. Tennyson and myself have most kindly and pleasant recollections of your brother and he must ever retain one of the foremost places among American guests who have done honour to their country and whom it is good for us to have known." The tone of this note suggests that there must have been fairly continuous correspondence after 1855. In all probability, here is another lamentable case of valuable, informative letters which have been lost or destroyed.

Tennyson's high regard for Tuckerman no doubt helped encourage him to continue writing poetry no longer as a humble disciple but as a writer confident that he could advance his poetic career, sure that Tennyson's opinion was ample authority for him to think of himself as an independent poet armed with a right sense of poetic worth and strong feeling and as a poet capable of creating works with his own individual stamp. His relationship with Tennyson provided, therefore, sufficient excitement to sustain Tuckerman as he resumed his serene life in Greenfield, walking through the woods and climbing to his familiar Poet's Seat to contemplate nature and to write his poems.

VII *First Publications*

"But view our Critic!"

Tuckerman's family now consisted of two children, Edward, who was born on June 29, 1848, and Hannah, born on March 29, 1853. In the spring of 1857 his "heart waited, trustfully serene,/ For the new blossom on [his] household-tree," and on May 7 the second son, Frederick, was born.[52] On May 12, 1857, Mrs. Tuckerman died of complications arising from childbirth and this sudden tragedy drew a heavy shade over the rest of Tuckerman's life. How deeply he felt her death is in the epitaph from the Lamentations of Jeremiah which he caused to be cut on her headstone: " 'Behold and see all ye that pass by, if there be any sorrow like unto my sorrow.' " As Jeremiah lamented the loss of his whole world in the fall of Jerusalem, so Tuckerman witnessed his own world collapse. His poetic monument, the heart of the sonnets in Part II, forms one of the most sensitive and profound memorials to grief in American literature. When Tuckerman privately printed his volume *Poems*, and early in 1861 sent out presentation copies, the ensuing correspondence became a valuable part of the literary history of the poet as well as a good barometer of literary taste in America of that time. All this material will be dealt with in a subsequent chapter.

Tuckerman spent a relatively busy spring and summer in 1861 as he kept track of reactions to his slim volume. In that year he must have been gratified by the favorable reception which "Rhotruda" received when it was printed in the *Atlantic*. The reviewer for the *Boston Evening Transcript* wrote that it "will attract special attention . . . it is the production of a new poet, but one whose exquisite genius must soon make him famous." Another reviewer thought the poem "was rugged and uneven in style, but withal not unpleasant." James T. Fields told Tuckerman that it was "liked exceedingly," and he was so enthusiastic that in June of 1862, ventured to print one of the few sonnets unrelated to the series which had appeared in the 1860 edition. The choice, "The starry flower, the flower-like stars that fade," was bold but unfortunate because Fields failed to realize that this sonnet made little sense without the one that followed it. Instead of receiving the sort of critical comment which his other work had elicited, Tuckerman now became the victim of some very harsh remarks and of two cruel parodies which bordered on the burlesque.

He pasted a notice from the Boston correspondent of the *Springfield Daily Republican* and clippings of the two parodies into a notebook. In addition, he kept a sonnet written in his defense plus a consolatory snippet which reads:

> It is the misfortune of excellence to be parodied.
> No one dreams of burlesquing shallow mediocrity.
> Gray's "Elegy" has often been parodied.

He could have added how often Tennyson had been so treated.

The reporter for the *Springfield Daily Republican* flatly stated that this sonnet was probably the worst one ever written and "liable to be printed among the curiosities of literature as such." One of the parodists attacked the sonnet because of its cloudy style. He saw

> Poor murdered language, laying stiff and stark;
> Words that have somehow lost their vital spark;
> As if the lexicon, in playful antic,
> Shook them as from a dice-box—new and old

and

> . . . like a pebble in a ring of gold,
> Lies a dead sonnet in the June *Atlantic*.

To an ultra-conservative reader such a position has some validity. The sonnet was enduring the treatment common to works which went beyond accustomed boundaries of mid-nineteenth-century subscribers to the *Atlantic*. But the second parody was in very poor taste, shabby and shameful. It revealed a false wit which reduced the parody to mockery:

> The starry flower, the flower-like stars that fade
> And brighten with the daylight and the dark,—

was parodied in these lines:

> The snowy flour, the flour-like snows that fade,
> The weekly wash, the work from dawn to dark,

and the writer proceeded to denigrate the Irish immigrant with

> . . . always remembering this,
> That home he reeleth, roaring, thrice-a-week
> Tippled O'Brien, in the midnight, *blue*!

These lines parody Tuckerman's

> . . . always remembering this,—
> His hand, who touched the sod with showers of gold,
> Stippled Orion on the midnight blue.

The sonnet written in Tuckerman's defense was signed "Julia." In it the author directed her remarks to the second parody, taking its writer to task for his "rough wit" and questioned if

"Cooks, pedants, Hobos" could appreciate anything at all. Her counter-parody ended with these lines:

> . . . always remembering this,
> His hand who made the sonnet all of gold—
> Makes the harsh ache and reiterance too.

Very soon after Tuckerman had weighed the critical comments following the 1860 edition, had noted the brief remarks about "Rhotruda," and had pondered the crude parodies, he decided to bring out a British edition. His motivation, as he had mentioned to Hawthorne, was that his work might win a more favorable reception from and be treated more gently by critics abroad. Witter Bynner thought that Tennyson may have influenced the decision, but there is no supporting evidence. A more plausible explanation is that James T. Fields had something to do with it. He was the foremost intermediary between British and American publishers and, as a friend of Tuckerman, could have arranged this venture. As has been noted, this London edition appeared in 1863; reaction to it both in England and in America is discussed in a later chapter.

Tuckerman did not express his personal feelings about the reception the volume had received, but he must have been firmly convinced that it would not achieve much success. Disappointment or even defeat did not hinder him from continuing his writing. After 1860 he wrote the three sonnet sequences, *The Cricket*, a few short poems, and some unfinished verse which remained unpublished during his lifetime. When the 1869 edition came out, there were no changes or additions; and it may be that he was completely unaware of its printing.

VIII   *The Final Years*

"Save tears and memory, all is gone"

The death of an infant daughter in 1848 and the loss of his wife in 1857, added to Tuckerman's propensity to melancholy, were enough sorrow for such a man. But he had more to endure as the war reached into Greenfield. Several of his townsmen had been killed in battle, and he grieved for them. The most cruel blow was the death of Colonel George D. Wells at South Cedar Creek in October, 1864.[53] In "G. D. W.," a posthumous work, he eulogizes his friend, whom he called the "River-God." Colonel Wells had been the leader of a group which had enjoyed excursions into the woods:

A little band of friends were we
Together still by steep and stream
We wander'd joyfully, and he
The leader of our faith and dream.

We broke the flower, and bow'd the weed,
The berries caught, the river quaff'd,
And if the world went wild indeed
Look'd in each others' eyes and laugh'd.[54]

By 1867 Tuckerman decided to quit Greenfield. The local newspaper reported that he had sold the house on Church Street and intended to spend a few years abroad.[55] In Boston it was believed that he wished to move to Concord. On August 25, Sophia Hawthorne wrote that her nephew, Horace Mann, wanted to sell his mother's house but it seems that Tuckerman preferred to buy the Hawthorne residence. In her letter Mrs. Hawthorne said that she had given up plans for a European trip and that it was "very pleasant to think of leasing it to a poet, and a friend of Mr. Hawthorne." Tuckerman wanted to buy the house, but Mrs. Hawthorne said, "We can never *sell* it, unless some great reverse of fortune should oblige us to do so."

However, during the following spring she renewed the subject. On April 5, 1868, she wrote: "I have now decided to *sell* the dear old Wayside, and before I say a word about it to anyone else, I offer it to you the Poet, and the friend of Mr. Hawthorne, because I cannot bear to have a stranger and a profane person possess it." Anxious to sell Wayside but reluctant to abandon its association with her husband, she thought Tuckerman would be an ideal buyer, who would keep alive all her memories of the place:

To think of you in Mr. Hawthorne's study—and preserving the aspen tree upon which he cut his cypher—and the woodbine he planted and watered, which he intended should climb to his study window, would be a pleasant thought to me. The footpath he wore with his feet on the summit of the wooded hill above the terraces—and the large white pine under which he liked to recline and listen to the sea song in the branches—while in May the grass was blue with large violets around him—I am sure you would truly appreciate. A part of that tree he burnt by accident, when trying to destroy the undergrowth around it. . . . There are a few charming paths, cut and good—and Mr. Hawthorne planted four hundred and fifty Norway spruces, which he selected in England—and there is a row of fine larches on what we call our larch avenue. I wish they could be in leaf before you walk along that avenue—but their effect could easily be imagined in leaf, though they are now sealed up.[56]

In a postscript she urged him to keep private her decision to sell Wayside, not wishing to have her intentions generally known until after he had made a decision.

Why Tuckerman should have wished to leave Greenfield is obscure. Perhaps the town held too much sadness for him; perhaps he wanted to be near his son, Edward, who was getting ready to enter Harvard College. The upshot was that Tuckerman changed his mind and decided to remain where he was. With his house sold, he moved into the American House, a hotel in the center of town. Hardly had he resettled when new calamity struck. In 1869, Edward, his eldest son, died in his twenty-first year. The next year, Tuckerman's aged mother passed away. Neither death is recorded in his poetry, but it may be that by now he had exhausted his strain of grief. *The Cricket,* one of his last works, was his final word and summation of his grief, his purpose in living, and his view of death. This poem is his real obituary.

A single paragraph in the *Greenfield Gazette* noted that Frederick Goddard Tuckerman died of heart disease at the age of fifty-two on May 9, 1873.[57] The notice added that "He lived a retired and secluded life among us," "was an excellent scholar, and had published several fine poems." He was buried in the Federal Street Cemetery in Greenfield in a grave between those of his wife and his eldest son. Cut into the stone are the opening lines of Sonnet XXXII, Part II: "Oh for the face and footstep!—Woods and shores/That looked upon us in life's happiest flush."

IX   *Withdrawal from Society*

"A part like Peto"

If the impression that Tuckerman was a recluse becomes the dominant one, then his life was lived in vain. It is true that he disengaged himself from society, but it is equally true that his poetry taken as a unit is the story of a man who strove to reconcile his lonely ways with more social ones and who ultimately succeeded in making the necessary adjustments so that in his last sonnets he could record a harmonious relationship between himself and the world about him.

There are some facts to support the position that Tuckerman was a virtual hermit. George S. Hillard and the reviewer in the New York *Tribune* referred to his reclusive ways. The poet's son, Frederick, said that his father "lived much in seclusion from the world."[58] Witter Bynner elaborated on this single sentence to suggest his agreement: "From 1857 till his own death, . . . Tuckerman became more of a recluse than ever . . . he appears to have remained away from human contacts, to have stayed by his flowers, his stars and his thoughts."[59] Bynner left some room for a readjustment in his appraisal by stating that, as Tuckerman grew older, he seemed "in heart and mind to have been drawn somewhat closer to humanity and its problems. Solitude and the recesses of his own existence had not finally severed him from solicitude for others."[60] This observation is correct.

His withdrawal from active participation in the literary and intellectual life of New England resulted in his being at best merely acquainted with some contemporaries. He knew Emerson on a personal basis, but with Channing or Thoreau he had no personal connection. Between 1861, when Tuckerman and Hawthorne had corresponded, and 1867-68, when Tuckerman and Mrs. Hawthorne were engaged in an exchange of letters about the possibility of his buying Wayside, the two writers might well have become good friends. In her correspondence, Mrs. Hawthorne refers to Tuckerman as the friend of her husband, which suggests a closer connection than existing factual evidence supplies.

He did not know Whitman, but he was early aware of his work and appreciated it enough to enter into his commonplace book a list of poems which included this notation: "Bardic Symbols—Whitman Elemental Drifts! Oh I wish—." When Tuckerman's sister was in Boston on one of her infrequent visits, she wrote to James Russell Lowell, inviting him to read and possibly review her book of poems, "Minor Chords"; and in her letter she added a note saying, "My brother Frederick Tuckerman I believe is an old friend of yours." There is nothing to substantiate this statement.

Intriguing as it may be to conjecture that Tuckerman knew Emily Dickinson, there is little support for such a possibility. The Dickinson family knew the Edward Tuckerman family which lived in Amherst, where Edward was professor of botany at Amherst College. Many letters passed between them, but there is not a single mention in any of them of the Greenfield poet. The poet's son Frederick, his wife and children, also knew the Dickinsons and several notes attest to a long and abiding friendship; but nothing in their correspondence forges a link between Tuckerman and Emily Dickinson.

T. W. Higginson was a good friend of Edward Tuckerman. He wrote from Newport that he "always dreamed of coming to Amherst" to see his friend and his "unseen correspondent Emily Dickinson."[61] He also knew Frederick Goddard Tuckerman when both were undergraduates at Harvard, but there is nothing in his correspondence to indicate that they had any relationship in adulthood.

With these three intermediaries it would seem possible that Emily Dickinson had heard of the poet who lived only twenty-five miles away. It is incredible that Tuckerman's poetry was never mentioned to her, and it is unlikely that his published volume did not come to her attention. Yet, all this is conjecture; and it must, therefore, be that they were strangers.

But the picture of Tuckerman's drifting away from humanity after 1857 into a self-made oblivion is not quite true. There is an accumulation of facts to refute this position. He lived physically close to his community. His home on Church Street was in the heart of the town and he had contact with what went on there. For example, Sonnets VI and VII, Part V, tell of visits to the lyceum with an old friend. On one of these visits

> . . . the town turned out and crammed the hall.
> And I, perhaps maliciously, made one
> To hear the lecture: I, who went to none,
> And an old friend with me, who went to all.

Bynner says that the poet made "occasional excursions to play pool with his fellow-townsmen in the public pool-hall." In connection with the founding of the Greenfield Library Association in 1855, Tuckerman's name is listed among the original donors and founders.[62] In 1861, he was so aroused by war issues that he delivered a speech on the Greenfield Common.

George B[agley], who heard about this event, wrote: "Your military ardour must have risen immensely to induce you to make a speech to the *hoi polloi* of Greenfield." Even if Tuckerman lived in some sort of retirement, he was not forgotten by his townsmen; they invited him to write the ode for the dedication of the Soldier's Monument on October 6, 1870. Thus, never completely cut off from friends or community life, he simply lived, as he so accurately put it, "Apart from friends, remote in misery." More precisely, he lived a private life.

Tuckerman's uneventful biography does not invite attention to his poetry, but his poetry calls attention to his life. The facts herein assembled give him a local habitation, and his poetry provides a name. Essentially, he wrote about himself and for himself. In the earliest manuscripts he labeled the two sonnet series published during his life, "Personal Sonnets" and the three posthumous ones deserve the same qualification. When the five series are considered as a whole, a spiritual biography unfolds in a language and a voice both rich and unique in American letters.

CHAPTER 2

Inner Biography:
'O dreamer in the Shadow!'

I *The First Twenty-eight Sonnets*

"The agony to know"

AUTOBIOGRAPHICAL ASPECTS in Tuckerman's poems are so clear and so striking that they call for considerable attention, not because they are rare or recondite but because they are so voluminous and apparent. Setting aside a handful of lyrics and narratives from his work, almost everything he wrote was subjective. The consistency and tenacity with which he pursued his self-preoccupation suggest that he possessed the rare ability to achieve a personal dichotomy which permitted him to regard himself objectively. He saw himself as clearly and as sharply as he observed the flowers, the plants, and the stars. He never wearied of examining and even fondling his moods, his feelings, and his thoughts. His stubborn disposition and his dogged determination to understand himself were relentless. As a result, his sonnets become a clear analysis and steady revelation of a troubled, perplexed mind intent on trying to make sense out of his life and to give it meaning.

Tuckerman knew exactly what he was doing and was aware that he would be misunderstood. As he told Hawthorne, his poems were written only for those who could understand.[1] Readers who dismissed his work as the melancholic outpourings of a self-pitying poet missed the whole point. He did not enjoy nursing his grief or courting futile regrets; he did, however, see the necessity to bring them out of personal darkness and to expose them to light. Unfortunately, most of his contemporaries read without understanding; but they may be partially excused because all of Tuckerman's work was unknown to them and their judgments had to be based on incomplete knowledge of it and, consequently, of the man. When all the sonnets and *The Cricket* are read in the light of his intention, the impression is gained of a remarkably strong man who fought against "quiet desperation" and frustration. His major writings coalesce into a full and detailed picture of one who could cast out grief, melancholy, and doubt and replace them with optimism, certainty, and faith. As he, himself, concluded, "But into order falls our life at last,/Though in the retrospection jarred and blent."[2]

His sonnets are almost a clinical report of this tremendous achievement. His removal to Greenfield and his withdrawal from society are symbolic of his moving out of himself in order to see himself more clearly as he strove for self-realization. Through his own efforts he struggled to bring into harmony the workings of nature, the role of the Creator, and his own place in relation to these forces. How he succeeded becomes the central theme of his inner biography.

The first sequence of twenty-eight sonnets, written before 1854, is given over entirely to an examination of doubt, indecision, and his "Margites" complex. He ranges across his youthful days to those of manhood in an effort to find the source of his disturbance. There is a steady hammering at his experience to force it to yield its meaning, if it has any. He becomes convinced that reason must be rejected in favor of faith and intuition if he is ever to understand his distress. The opening sonnet asks if there is any worth or value in his "dim fancies, cares and fears" or to what avail is the "swan's voice" and "great flight" if unheard or unseen. Even if the poet's and the swan's voices speak and are unheard, they still have worth, else "God were not God, whom knowledge cannot know." The second and third sonnets continue the subject with "this belief held like a blade" and with his resolve to carry it to "the heart/ Of that dark doubt in one collected blow."

But, even as he musters his force, the strength of his conviction weakens before the opposing power of doubt; and, sinking into defeat, he, like Dante looking on the Ancients, envies those who have been successful in clearing away doubts. By comparison, his "proudest thoughts do seem . . . a barren gleam/Among the immortal stars." His voice of conscience chides him for his temerity in trying to answer queries which demand greater experience than he now possesses, and he is overcome by its scolding and by a realization of his inadequacies. Regretting his lost youth and fully aware of his present plight, he reports:

> . . . Apart I stepped;
> And while the laugh and song went lightly by,
> In the wild bushes I sat down and wept.

The search goes back to his youth. Sonnets IV, V, and VI form a trio in which he says that he has lost the certainty of youthful knowledge and is now without light to chase away the gloom of "unfulfilled yet unrelinquished sins/That hedge [him] in." He feels that he is "Wide of the way, nor sure to turn or pause"; he cannot understand and enjoy the glory of nature so long as his thirst for knowledge is unslaked. He is

> . . . as the dim pampas plain,
> Hoary with salt and gray with bitter weed,
> Sees the vault blacken, feels the dark wind strain,
> Hears the dry thunder roll, and knows no rain.

Lost in his own vague thoughts, he turns from the quietness of his frustration with "a groping hand to rend the dark," to call "entangled in the night" filled with vague "wind and voices"; but his voice produces sound without meaning. The darkness and sense of despair in Sonnet VI are sustained with the search for direction as he moves into the haunting region of Sonnet VII:

> Dank fens of cedar, hemlock-branches gray
> With tress and trail of mosses wringing-wet,
> Beds of the black pitch-pine in dead leaves set
> Whose wasted red has wasted to white away,
> Remnants of rain and droppings of decay,—
> Why hold ye so my heart nor dimly let
> Through your deep leaves the light of yesterday,
> The faded glimmer of a sunshine set?
> Is it that in your blindness, shut from strife,
> The bread of tears becomes the bread of life?
> Far from the roar of day, beneath your boughs
> Fresh griefs beat tranquilly and loves and vows
> Grow green in your gray shadows, dearer far
> Even than all lovely lights and roses are?

Sonnets VIII and IX resume the thoughts of youth, and in them life is a journey down an ever widening stream until the banks spread so far apart that there are no landmarks. In desperation, the voyager resorts to the futility of finding guidance in the "purple air" as "life alone circles out flat and bare." In Sonnet IX, bereft of youth and adrift in the river of Sonnet VIII, the poet says that, despite the loss of guideposts, he must persist in his quest even though he "wander silently and brood among/Dead graves and tease the sunbreak and the cloud/For import." He asks if it might be better to follow blindly the thoughts of others, but he almost immediately rejects the idea with the stubborn hope that he may "Come into light at last" and, like biblical Saul, "hear a voice."

Sonnet X interrupts his musings to tell of a youth who had met an untimely death. As the poet meditates upon the "upper chamber in a darkened house/Where, ere his footsteps reached ripe manhood's brink" and as he dreams about the place with its "terror and anguish," he abruptly shakes off the gloomy reverie to resume the thoughts previously expressed. He asks,

> What profits it to me, though here allowed
> Life, sunlight, leisure, if they fail to urge
> Me to due motion or myself to merge
> With the onward stream, too humble, or too proud?

He returns in the last six lines of Sonnet IX to bring to mind again the young man's death. In combining these two sonnets, he fuses this meaningless death with his own meaningless grief as he confesses,

> . . . I coldly creep
> By summer farms and fields, by stream and steep,
> Dull and like one exhausted with deep sleep.

Sonnets XII and XIII begin with a renewal of energy and "A cry for strength, for strength and victory," but, as the cry goes unheeded, he sighs for those days of youth when he fought with great imagined courage "amid the mullein-stalks" pushing "the battle backward, rank on rank/Fallen in the sword-swing of his stormy hand." Awakening from this daydream, he finds himself lost like one who is on a foreign shore where the "heavy land-wash break"; and, "apart from friends, remote in misery," he can only "brood on pain and find in heaven no sign." Although he is "left alone to die" and "hears his parting comrades' jeers and scoffs," he still retains some hope because he sees "through mists that hinder and deform,/The dewy stars of home,—." His emotional isolation arises as much from the attitude and actions of his former friends as it does from his own condition.

Sonnets XIV, XV, and XVI are a short, dramatic narrative designed to contrast his withdrawal from a hostile society with his separation of another kind. In the first of these three sonnets, his friend, a man who "with a wise direction ruled himself" and who could "reap/From hardest things a consequence and use," is shaken from his security by the sudden death of his young bride:

> And yet this friend of mine, in one small hour
> Fell from himself and was content to weep
> For eyes love-dark, red lips, and cheeks in hues
> Not red but rose-dim, like the jacinth-flower!

Once she had "turned to him as to a god of old" and had given "herself as but a little thing," but now her death has left the friend with nothing more than "the wild grief of unperfected years." The poet begins the third sonnet with the strong assurance that nature can assuage the grief of his friend just as, with "consenting colour," she heals wounds caused by lightning and covers their ugliness with "mosses green and dank." But such confidence in the healing power of nature is misplaced because, while she can heal the physical, she cannot touch the bereaved one's heart. In a situation beyond nature's power, he now "breathes apart, to daily drink/In tears the bitter ashes of his love."

The next four sonnets continue the exploration of the relationship of man and nature, with the poet weighing his own idle state with that of the toiler in the field. Sonnet XVII begins with a country preacher warning, "Lo, Death is at the doors . . . with blows!" The last five lines and the first two lines of Sonnet XVIII make reference to his own "feverish sense" which hears "the stars tick audibly." The preacher's loud voice is dim when compared to the "wind's low surge" which is magnified into "a Niagara of sound." The toiler is urged to ignore the preacher's idle speculation and to do his planting well

> . . . That so may spring
> From the deep grain a goodlier growth and kind,
> Unstirred of heats that blast, of frosts that bind,
> Nor swept aside, ere the seed catch, by wing
> Of casual shower nor any chance of wind.

In Sonnet XIX the poet balances the value of his own actions with the work of the farmer; at this point he thinks the farmer's work more valuable:

> Yet vain, perhaps, the fruits our care applaud.
> If the fore-fate decree the harvest fat,
> Why should we mind this thing or matter that,
> To sift the seed and blow the chaff abroad?
> But doubt not so the giver to defraud
> Who will accuse thy labour. Spend, nor slack
> Of thy best strength and sweetness too, till God
> With a full hand and flowing pay thee back.
> Behold, on rolling zone and zodiac
> The spray and scatter of his bounty flung.
> And what canst thou, to whom no hands belong
> To hasten by one hour the morning's birth
> Or stay one planet at his circle hung,
> In the great flight of stars across the earth?

Sonnet XX reveals his belief that nature never satisfies man's craving and yearning for God, which have been part of his very existence everywhere and in every time. If the farmer is the worthiest of God's creatures and if the poet sees no difference between the "son of toil" and "Ophion, earliest of the gods," then what remains for the poet? He answers his own question in Sonnet XXI: the only thing left for him is to beg God's mercy. A tearful entreaty, this sonnet is his wish to be guided to "His footstool." The poet has, in effect, rejected nature because of her indifference to man's real needs; and, in Sonnet XXII, he cries out at such indifference and cruelty: "But sweep, sweep on, wild blast! Who bids thee stay?" This strong, dramatic rejection of nature is the climax of Part I. He sees that there is value in strength—a strength he, apparently, still lacks.

Sonnets XXIII and XXIV are distinguished by the quiet dignity they give to Anna, his wife, as she brings solace to a dying "fair young mother." He is proud that "Anna did not flee/ To grief or fear, nor lies in slumber dull." If these sonnets are only dreams, he says let it be so; for dreams have their worth in the search for truth: ". . . surely truth has beamed/Oft from the gate of dreams upon the brain." He emphasizes the need for faith in the tireless search for serenity and certainty. He wonders why "men doubt and balance and disdain,/Where she, the gentler spirit, seeks to skim/Light from the vague." "The

gentler spirit" is Faith; and, to firmly establish its importance
in life, he ends the sonnet with a varied gallery of notable
women from history, mythology, and the Bible, who had exhibited a faith so strong that it serves as an ideal and as an
inspiration. In four tumultuously charged lines, he brings together Manoah's wife, Deborah, Actia, Arlotte, and Mandané.
In the next sonnet, he searches for faith in nature. He prods his
memory

> . . . to bring the days forever done
> And call the mountains, where our love begun
> And the dear happy woodlands dipped in dew
> And pore upon the landscape, like a book,
> But cannot find her.

The last three sonnets bring the whole sequence to its close.
He is convinced that nature cannot be trusted as a true guide
since she "breathes contradiction where she seems most clear."
Here he is on sure ground because he knows that he has the
gift of fathoming her secrecies. He had, for example, thought
himself "possessed of Nature's ear" when

> The night-hawk blew his horn at sunny noon;
> And in the rainy midnight I have heard
> The ground-sparrow's long twitter from the pine
> And the cat-bird's silver song, the wakeful bird
> That to the lighted window sings for dawn.

The contradictions in nature make "a haunting theme for anger,
joy, or tears" because when "hunted home, behold its opposite."
Thus, he who puts full reliance in nature will learn to his regret
that "hopes are fears,/And love is woe."

The final sonnet is his assertion that God is the true source
of all men's certainty. Neither nature nor thought "the recon-
cilement holds." The meaning of life is with God, and God can
be reached not through reason, not through nature, but only
through exercise of faith. He recapitulates the three aspects:
"The agony to know" belongs to the poet; "the grief," to those
who have suffered; and, the "bliss of toil" to the worker in the
fields, who has a sense of usefulness and worth. Under such
conditions, the poet must rely on faith as his inner voice com-
mands:

No more thy meaning seek, thine anguish plead;
But leaving straining thought and stammering word,
Across the barren azure pass to God:
Shooting the void in silence, like a bird,—
A bird that shuts his wings for better speed.

These twenty-eight sonnets, which comprise Part I, lay bare one view of Tuckerman's inner life. His early religious background and his deep interest in the workings of nature clash; as a result, he is at war with himself. But he succeeds in bringing about a temporary inner peace by rejection of an indifferent nature that must perform her work inexorably and blindly. In these sonnets he explains to his own satisfaction that the more one studies nature at work, the more one must come to accept her contradictory ways. A serious student of nature, sensitive to her activities, and privy to many of her secrets, he knows that his understanding is inadequate to go behind and beyond these contradictions to arrive at peace among his own clashing emotions. He was heavy-hearted at this impasse but never light-headed. Adamant and unyielding where he could not see or understand and refusing to accept blindly popular notions, he plowed his intellectual furrow as deep and as straight as did the "son of toil" he so admired and envied.

In rejecting nature as a guide to life, he is not casting her completely aside. He is too much of a realist to do that. What he expounds is that the total mystery of nature is beyond his comprehension and that man's certainty rests in God. He does not assume a Deistic position but believes that God permeates all nature and at the same time is above, beyond, and superior to it. There is nothing very original in this judgment. What is memorable is his independent and orderly thought couched in graceful and exciting sonnets. His method of attacking his personal problem is Baconian: "If we begin with certainties we shall end in doubts; but if we begin with doubts, and are patient in them, we shall end in certainties." Tuckerman's approach fits this dictum exactly. The queries posed in Sonnet I were answered with certainty in Sonnet XXVIII. With the mind of a scientist and the heart of a poet, he reveals how nature thwarts man's insistence to know her absolutely. Her seeming cruelty which brings about unwarranted human sorrow and her lavish ways of concealment leave him no choice but to abandon his "straining thought" and swiftly and directly fly to God.[3]

In variant versions of the manuscripts, the only constant factor is the ordering of the sonnets. They were arranged into a tight unit so organically and so skilfully wrought that disruption of their order would destroy the whole series. All twenty-eight sonnets are artfully linked so that their chain of thought possesses a uniform strength able to withstand any shock and stress. The devices employed to create such sure and reliable linkage are varied. Tuckerman may permit a sonnet to reach its end without punctuation and force the reader to continue to the next one to capture the content, as in Sonnets II and III. At times the transition is borne by the opening phrase, as may be noted in Sonnet XXIV in which "Perhaps a dream" refers to the preceding sonnet and establishes the true relationship. The flow of narrative serves as the connective in Sonnets XIV, XV, and XVI. Occasionally, the device is less obvious. For example, Sonnet X at first may appear as a digression, but it is integrated into the structure of Sonnet XI, in which the first eight lines refer to Sonnet IX and the remainder to Sonnet X. In this intricate way the unity is preserved.

This kind of linking is augmented by a secondary one. Controlling images occur and recur like variations on a musical theme to keep the whole series unified. An image of battle in Sonnet II is matched by a counterpart in Sonnet XII and again in Sonnet XXV; the insistent voice of conscience is heard in Sonnets III, IX, XIX, and XXVIII. Both types of connectives bear witness to Tuckerman's conscious desire to have the sonnets form an unbreakable unit in the delineation of his quest.

II *Delineation of Grief; Renewal of Faith*

"These offspring of my sorrow"

Although Part II is primarily devoted to the memory of Tuckerman's wife, its true theme is not so much his lamenting her death as it is the elevation of the human spirit from the depths of personal despair to a level where grief, rid of tears and senseless moaning, attains grace, dignity, and hope. Faith, embraced in Part I, is the agency through which the poet escapes from the self-pity which threatens to engulf him. Just as Part I moves from a mood of despair to one of certitude, Part II goes from gloom to optimism. During the journey, the poet passes through regions of morbidity and pathos, but he extricates himself to avoid permanent despondency.

He approaches his subject warily, almost reluctantly. The opening sonnet is a pastoral prelude comparing the farm boy's toil with his own; and, in the first half of Sonnet II, he asserts that both perform "great workings." Suddenly, in line eight, he introduces a major note, the revelation of his wife's death, whose eternal sleep he compares with that of the farm boy's "still strong sleep, till but the east is red." He develops the theme by suggesting that his own grief is like that of a man who, looking from a height to his home sees it ablaze, and returning, finds "a smouldering pit." This catastrophe leads him to observe that ". . . grief finds solace faint in others' ills/ And but in her own shadow loves to go" and that his sorrow is so personal and blinding that nothing outside of itself has meaning. The destroyed home burns more deeply into the spirit than if

> The sun, from his high place descending slow,
> Should over the autumn landscapes brood and burn
> Till all the vales were tinder, and their crags,
> Apt to the touch of fire, Hephaestian hills.

Sonnets V, VI, VII, and VIII work closely toward an understanding of the nature of personal grief. In Sonnet V, he envies the uncomplicated man who "gathers his bread by run-sides, rocks and groves," who ". . . drinks from rivers of a thousand soils." Such a guileless man can listen to the poet's thoughts and plainly say, "Your brain is planet-struck." The next sonnet starts with a plea for acceptance of the judgment of the simple but terminates with the imposing thought that "perfect grief, like love, should cast out fear." Inane comments from "those who stoop and peer/To pick with sharpened fingers for a flaw" in his perfect grief are far worse than "surgery rough as that/ Which, hammer and chisel in hand, at one sharp blow/Strikes out the wild tooth from a horse's jaw."

To show that grief can be felt only on a personal basis, the poet tells of a friend whose wide interests ranged from the garden to the stars, from "bards, heroes, prophets, Homers, Hamilcars" to angels and devils. The friend had so simplified nature and art that both could be understood within the intimacy and confines of a garden. In the next sonnet, the poet and the friend wander in the woods where the latter asserts that "thought is free" and that beauty is everywhere. The placid tenor of the narrative is abruptly broken in Sonnet IX, which opens with a statement that "swift calamity" has come to the friend. The poet withholds details to contrast this calamity with his own serenity as he awaits the birth of his child. Then, after a general observation that "flowers and gods and quaint philosophy" do not relieve grief, he tells the nature of the "swift calamity" and adds to it his own sudden loss: "Can spring return to him a brother's face,/Or bring my darling back to me—to me?"

The first nine sonnets form an elaborate preface to Tuckerman's poetic monument to the memory of his wife. He tells of the birth of the child, of the death of its mother, and of his own changed condition. He stands "like a charred and fire-hardened trunk,/To break the axe's edge of time and fate!" No sooner has he established the source, the cause, and the effect of his present grief than he introduces a note of hope. Sonnet XI is a dim light of comfort as elusive as "the witchlight of the reedy river-shore." Displeased with his verse which cannot cope adequately with "life, love, experience, art,/Fused into grief," he reviews his existence. It has been one of "high desire, . . . faint accomplished deed,/Unuttered love and loss"; but, unwilling to surrender to his self-disesteem, he reads "the blotted page, re-turning leaf and leaf" and partially deludes himself that the words adequately express his emotions. His lingering upon his verse and his pampering of his grief remind him of a lover whose unfettered mind adorns his beloved with strange flowers and rare gems. This image lures him to recall in Sonnet XIV, a memorable day at the seashore with Anna. But this pleasant evocation loses its joy in a note of instability; it responds to "shuddering play," "trembling turf," "surging surf," and "simmering suds."

Anxious to escape to solid ground from such unsure footing, he meditates upon the idea that nothing can survive when love is absent. Twin-Sonnets XV and XVI portray two aspects of Anna's beauty personified in the twins, Gertrude and Gulielma; the first, representing physical beauty; the second, spiritual beauty:[4]

Gertrude and Gulielma, sister-twins,
Dwelt in the valley at the farm-house old;
Nor grief had touched their locks of dark and gold
Nor dimmed the fragrant whiteness of their skins:
Both beautiful, and one in height and mould;
Yet one had loveliness which the spirit wins
To other worlds,—eyes, forehead, smile and all,
More softly serious than the twilight's fall.
The other—can I e'er forget the day
When, stealing from a laughing group away,
To muse with absent eye and motion slow,
Her beauty fell upon me like a blow?—
Gertrude! with red flowerlip, and silk black hair!
Yet Gulielma was by far more fair!

Under the mountain, as when first I knew
Its low black roof and chimney creeper-twined,
The red house stands; and yet my footsteps find,
Vague in the walks, waste balm and feverfew.
But they are gone: no soft-eyed sisters trip
Across the porch or lintels; where, behind,
The mother sat,—sat knitting with pursed lip.
The house stands vacant in its green recess,
Absent of beauty as a broken heart.
The wild rain enters; and the sunset wind
Sighs in the chambers of their loveliness
Or shakes the pane—and in the silent noons
The glass falls from the window, part by part,
And ringeth faintly in the grassy stones.

This prolonged mood of grief, very close to self-pity, cannot endure indefinitely because "pain, fear, heart-break, woes and wars/Have natural limit." Eventually they must give way to the "splendour of the light." The change that has overtaken him since his wife had died is like the changes which have occurred in the woods around Greenfield and among his neighbors. In Sonnet XVIII he sees that the woodlands have been cut by man and destroyed by fire; as a result, "the hunter's trail and trap-path is forgot." The growth of the village has driven away the dove and the deer; and, where the wolf-bait once hung from the bush, a house now stands. These intrusions into nature recall another kind of human inroad. In Sonnet XIX he re-creates the Deerfield massacre and Shays's Rebellion and finds it difficult to reconcile these violent events with his own changes. In

Sonnet XX he says, "O hard endeavour, to blend in with these/ Dark shadings of the past a darker grief." Disasters in nature and killings among men will somehow fade; personal sorrow lingers "through the slow years" and keeps fresh "each tone, each look of love, each syllable,/With lips that work, with eyes that overwell."

Intimations of hope and optimism begin to supplant his sorrow. He dreams Anna is being carried out to sea, and he yearns to follow. As he stands on the jetty watching her ship disappear, his only thought is that "Knowledge must bring relief"; and, when a wave breaks and sprays him, he shudders and turns away. This dream carries over into the next sonnet in which he watches the ship again and assures Anna,

> . . . Thou scarce canst fail to find,
> O desolate one, the morning breaking white,
> Some shore of rest beyond the labouring wave.

He now realizes that, if his wife has found rest, his grief should cease. His mourning takes a turn; now it is not directed to her but to his own lamentable condition:

> Ah, 'tis for this I mourn: too long I have
> Wandered in tears along life's stormy way
> Where, day to day, no haven or hope reveals.

Sonnet XXIII deals with the idea that the spirit's deep sadness may be pierced by truths which are "unapprehended, grand, remote." Man bows before their power without feeling them; they are too distant and too sublime to minister to spiritual needs. From the inaccessibility of the asterisms, he tries the opposite pole by looking to the town and to its inhabitants as possibly the most ready sources of human understanding. Throughout this poetic memorial, Tuckerman is trying to work his way out of the gloom. The road is long and torturous, but almost imperceptibly he manages to advance toward the light. Sonnets XXIV and XXV confirm what he has long suspected: the town is "alien and sad, the wreck of perished dreams." He abandons it to appease his anger by crying senselessly to the "unmoved skies." Town gossip is abhorrent; its pettiness and its concern with trivia are without meaning.

Unable to find a road which leads to inner peace, he is lost in indifference and in lassitude. With "vacant heart and brain" he sees no forward purpose in life, but he cannot accept defeat because he still retains the belief that life, even if it is worthless, must still be preserved. In the midst of this emotional agitation, his voice of conscience

> Loud on the ear her homely message sends,
> "Ere the sun plunge, determine. Up, awake,
> And for thy sordid being make amends.
> Truth is not found by feeling in the pocket,
> Nor wisdom sucked from out the fingers' end!"[5]

Shocked by the harsh command, he angrily replies,

> To idle time indeed, to moan our moan
> And then go shivering from a folded gate,
> Broken in heart and life, exheredate
> Of all we loved!

Slowly he moves out of his pitiable state and compares himself to a sick man just emerging from a long illness. He rides "on the first soft waves of slumber's calm" and imagines himself once more amid New England flowers or under Canadian skies. This "happy trance" is a prelude to recovery; for the first time, he fathoms the "prophetic woe" he once had encountered but could not comprehend.

Sonnets XXXI through XXXIV are the poet's fullest expression of his sorrow, but in them he recognizes that grief must eventually yield to happiness. This sequence begins with a scene in which his tranquil mood is matched by the quiet of "the low rain" when "no tempests rave"; he points to Anna's grave and looks "on the sweeping corn and the surging rye,/And with every gust of wind [his] heart goes by!" Unable to maintain restraint, he indulges in one final outburst of uncontrollable lamentation, crying "From the heart's heart, gathering more and more/Blindness and strangling tears."

On a still dark night as he sits writing, he feels the presence of two spirits. A strange voice asks, "Wherefore doth he weep and fear?"—and a familiar voice replies, "His heart is dimmed and drowned/With grief." In his imagination, he feels the latter bend down to kiss him; but, at that very moment, he hears the morning scream of the cock and the striking of the morning bell. The vision fades, and he listens to the dying sounds. Sonnet

XXXIV is a commentary on this vision that has given him strength and assurance that fear has been vanquished by love.

> My Anna! Though thine earthly steps are done,
> Nor in the garden nor beside the door
> Shall I behold thee standing any more,
> I would not hide my face from light nor shun
> The full completion of this worldly day.
> What though beside my feet no other one
> May set her own to walk the forward way,
> I will not fear to take the path alone,
> Loving for thy sake things that cheer and bless,
> Kind words, pure deeds, and gentlest charities.
> Nor will I cease to hold a hope and aim
> But, prophet-like, of these will make my bread
> And feed my soul at peace; as Esdras fed
> On flowers, until the vision and the glory came.

He has successfully traversed his personal Slough of Despondency; he confidently asserts that his thoughts about Anna have been so changed and so glorified that he can search for happiness again. Clearly and boldly, he announces that happiness can be found in "pure young hearts" and he looks to Anna "To hear her laugh again and feel her lips/Kiss from [his] brow the heavy thoughts away."

In Sonnet XXXVI, with perfect serenity and dignity, he looks to the ideal day

> Of restoration, when in fields divine,
> And walking as of old, thy hand in mine,
> By the still waters we may softly stray!

The self-assurance, laboriously and tearfully won, and the newly revived faith carefully sought, end Part II. Tuckerman had planned this biblical-sounding sonnet as the final one in Part II; but, in all the manuscripts and in all the editions before 1931, he used an unnumbered sonnet as an epilogue. In the 1931 edition, this sonnet is numbered and is made an integral part of the sequence. But, the assurance, confidence, and tranquillity of Sonnet XXXVI is emotionally the correct one to end the series because it asserts unmistakably the optimism he hoped to attain. Left unnumbered as he had indicated, the last sonnet serves admirably as the epilogue or *l'envoi*; for in it

he presents Part II to God as a tribute for the new life he feels
he has been granted:

> As Eponina brought, to move the king
> In the old day, her children of the tomb
> Begotten and brought forth in charnel gloom,
> To plead a father's cause, so I too bring
> Unto thy feet, my Maker, tearfully,
> These offspring of my sorrow, hidden long
> And scarcely able to abide the light.
> May their deep cry, inaudible, come to thee
> Clear through the cloud of words, the sobs of song,
> And sharper than that other's pierce thine ears—
> That so each thought, aim, utterance, dark or bright,
> May find thy pardoning love more blest than she
> Who joyful passed with them to death and night,
> With whom she had been buried nine long years!

III *Personal Sonnets of Hope*

"Let me give something!"

Tuckerman's intellectual and emotional struggles, so minutely
described in Parts I and II, are only two aspects of his character. The three posthumous sonnet sequences, written between
1864 and 1872, are as autobiographical as the earlier ones; but
there is less urgency in them to find immediate answers to the
vague doubts and quick solace for his grief. Instead, there is a
steady progression hopefully leading toward triumph over
the infirmities which dominated the subject matter of the earlier
sonnets. Tuckerman had apparently accepted his warring nature,
was willing to endure it, and was content to brood over it in a
general way. As a result, these later sequences are rather loosely
connected and free from the petulant impatience to immediately
solve the riddle of existence. He now views life on a less personal basis, but the fundamental problems have not changed:
he is still a troubled man.

Acceptance of his lot and an understanding of his place within
the human condition establish the tone and temper of Part III.
Alone, as he reads a dull book on a cloudy day, a sudden burst
of sunshine and the song of a bird distract him. By the time
he had left his house, the sun and the bird had vanished. Disappointed, he ". . . turned again and, entering with a groan,/

Sat darkly down to Dagoraus Whear." This simple example of nature's vagaries is developed in the next sonnet, which illustrates how "Nature, in her mood, pushes or pulls/At her caprice." Notwithstanding, he begins to consider the idea that she works for the benefit of all. Ships use the rivers as a means of transportation; gulls use them as guides into the hills. Her impersonality is further considered in Sonnet III. She never works for man's benefit alone, and the man "who dreams but on himself" and creates his own gloom can never find peace in nature until he becomes a "trustful child who on her heart [has] lain." He insists that she is benevolent and, despite her seeming inhospitable ways, is like "an embracing Friend."

The confident state of mind indicates how far he has advanced from the self-centered attitudes of Part I. If nature is a cosmic parent, then the poet is content to accept the role of a child. "Touched and smoothed" by "the great Bestower," he recalls the innocent play of childhood and the happy days when he walked along the seashore with Anna. He lingers over these delightfully nostalgic scenes because they seem proof that somehow nature's goodness will prevail.

Sonnets VIII and IX sum up the quiet confidence which has driven from his mind those doubts and fears that once had haunted him. Now he sees that everything falls into its proper place if man has patience and insight. The jarring events of earlier years have become a useless catalogue. He is free from his own

> Broken ambition, love misplaced or spent
> Too soon, and slander busy with the past;
> Sorrows too sweet to lose, or vexing joy.

Up to this point, Tuckerman appears to be leading his mind into a self-made Paradise; but he stops short of entering. He is not ready for complete submission; he is still a man bearing the scars of sadness and grief. In Sonnet X, he realizes that his thoughts are still half-shaped and his heart still joyless; but, instead of being meek and helpless, he sees himself rugged and enduring as a

> . . . high rock beneath whose base the sea
> Has wormed long caverns, like my tears in me:
> And hard like this I stand.

The next four sonnets are digressive and form a complete sequence by themselves. Once, Tuckerman had planned to let them stand alone; but he finally decided to incorporate them into this larger sequence—perhaps as leavening for his insistent and serious theme.[6] The final sonnet of this part gathers into a single sheaf all the confidence he had gained. In this forthright declaration of inner security and victory, he proudly asserts, "But death and dread responsibility/I hardly fear tonight or feel at all."

Strong evidence of his intellectual growth dominates the fourth part, which consists of ten sonnets. He has virtually rid himself of self-pity and has arrived at that point in his inner biography where he can further explore and chart the vast entangling and warring regions of thought, inspiration, and God. To better view these, he withdraws to a height from which to look "along the horizon darkening far" to envision places filled with "vague tumult, lights of woe, and moving war." He tries to understand the nature of the conflict by considering each part of it singly. For him thought is embodied in contemporary science, which is so confident of its own supremacy and so concerned with its own problems that it brushes aside the arrows of inspiration. He sees clearly that science will eventually be beaten by the very inspiration it scorns and that these two must ally to pierce nature's mysteries. Joined in harmony, they can succeed because inspiration provides fire to the mind; science, alone, is blind, but inspiration "as lightning instantly enlighteneth." He goes a step further by adding a third dimension: once science and inspiration have united, their combined force still needs the assistance of Divine Power. When all three are joined, the wilderness of human existence may be cleared away. Ultimate success depends upon this triple alliance, but in it God must be the strongest power. Tuckerman believes that "In man's extremity/God lends the light we use." God's function is to provide not only the light for thought and the fire for inspiration but also the strength for action. Action is the mental discipline which prevents trifling with time and wallowing in self-indulgence. From his own experience, he can warn others who lack action to "shun the reveries of voluptuous thought,/Day-musings, the floralia of the heart/And vain imaginations."

For the first time, Tuckerman has moved completely away from preoccupation with his own problems; he has come to recognize that a full life is impossible within the tight circle of personal existence. In Sonnet V he continues to urge acceptance of God and assails "believers for the nonce" who must trip at "absolute heaven and drop at once/In the red gulf." Acceptance of Divine Power does more than dignify work and provide hope: it is the source of love, a force capable of lifting man near the angelic state and, at the same time, of preserving benevolence and compassion for all mankind. Although his life has been shattered by personal tragedy, he reveals that he has fully recovered from the intense grief he described in the earliest sonnets; now he refuses to believe that life is futile. Hard as it is to accept this belief, his intuition informs him that, even if evil exists and often so masks itself that it is indistinguishable from good, there always "abides the good."

In Sonnet IX he leaves his concern with general humanity to mark changes which have taken place in Greenfield. Where once the Indian roamed, trains now run and factories rise. Sure that industrial progress cannot be stemmed and that its encroachments on nature are inevitable, he refuses to vex himself. Instead of fulminating against them, he turns away and walks through the woods "searching strange plants to medicine [his] mood." The final sonnet is an expression of great triumph, for he has so successfully re-ordered his life that he is willing— even anxious—to share his knowledge of the wonders and secrets of nature. The ordeal of grief, the frustrations of unresolved problems have been mastered; shared life and experience give real meaning to existence. His true work, he believes, is to observe and to record the workings of nature; he says that they are of no value when hoarded. Thus, he closes this sequence with a cordial invitation to the reader to join him on his expeditions, when he will gladly reveal the marvels he has discovered. "Then come/With me betimes," he invites, promising to show wonders even more enchanting than "the worm that, touched, a twig-like semblance takes"; than the "spermal odour of the barberry flower"; than the invisibility of the "twirling spider"; than the sour taste in the leaf of the "little chick-wintergreen star." He wants to take the reader by the hand and in the dawn show him the wonders that may be encountered in the search for "earliest flowers." Such an invitation from a man who is supposed to be a recluse is a guarantee that he has matured over the years. This part of the poetic journal provides the strongest possible evidence that Tuckerman's spiritual indecisions and social weaknesses, so marked in Parts I and II, have been overcome. Fears and doubts assail all men; therefore, all men must contribute something to allay human distress.

The change in his thinking continues into Part V. The first three sonnets dwell on the idea that nature's ways are beyond human comprehension and that understanding her activities calls for divine aid because nature's necessity is to work through God's "invention and authority." If man can exercise patience and observe nature closely, he will eventually see her stirring at his feet. Despite man's intellect, nature guards her vast mysteries, the greatest of these being man himself.

Human efforts are not to be despised. He sees the man of science amazed and frightened by his ability to unveil some of nature's hidden workings; but, even while pursuing his scientific investigations, he is still a mortal who, probing deeply into the mysteries of vast heavens, is startled by the meaning of a mere word. Tuckerman, who continues to think about science, doubts that it can ever master the universe but is aware that it can do much to build "towns, cables, cars and ships." While he is contemplating the work of the scientist, he finds his own of equal worth: both poet and scientist search nature through different means. The scientist "counts his course in truth by vigorous steps"; the poet mounts toward truth adding "crag to crag."

The abuse of knowledge is the theme of Sonnets VI and VII. He narrates two experiences at the local lyceum to illustrate the point. At one meeting the visiting lecturer came to enlighten ignorance but succeeded in "illuminating his own"; at the other, the speaker was a spellbinder whose senseless harangue brought strong men to tears and women to ecstasy by means of "a rant of phrase and metaphor." Tuckerman says that such charlatans will always be abroad but that he is under no obligation to clutter his mind with their popular nonsense.

Satisfied with his resolution of the problem of the relationships of thought, inspiration, and God, the poet moves from the world of general ideas to his private life to give expression to his thoughts on beauty. Initially he had been concerned with the concept of beauty only as it is manifest in nature, but later he came to consider it a vital element in human existence.

Sonnets VIII, IX, and X represent his latest thinking on the subject. The spiritual and intellectual beauty that he once saw in the Gertrude-Gulielma sonnets in Part II is now transformed into a simple, specific picture he saw from a train window as he "rode on to the wide city, loud and drear." In the first two poems, he intensifies the idea that human beauty extends and emanates to touch "all objects with transfiguring power." A plain cottage in a vale can become a "sweet kingdom" in the hills of Ule if beauty is present. This view of earthly beauty brings to his mind the beauty of Anna, a beauty exalted by death which lends a new dimension to worldly, ideal beauty because it rises superior to the ugliness seen in "clouded looks of hate, the harrowing eyes."

These two sonnets barely suggest but surely intimate that Tuckerman's mind has begun to encompass the idea of death. In the first, death is neither sordid nor sad; it is a means of reunion with Anna. In the second, the same idea dominates; it is a form of certainty of permanence beyond life, as illustrated by the legend of Phadimus and Tantalus. The final quartet of sonnets in Part V moves closer and closer to his explication of its meaning. As an escape from life, it has no value; its true sense is in the thought that the release from this life makes way for a newer one. He sees that time and casualties of war have reduced the number of his friends and acquaintances in Greenfield; and, inevitably, he senses his own death to be impending. He feels that it is a "new awakening"; as a result, his whole manner changes from that of the ineffectual mourner, or dream-laden romantic, to that of a donor of hope and inspiration. These hopes are his legacy, and the dominant cry is "Let me give something!" Perhaps all he can really bequeath is part of himself. He can leave a memorial in his poetry.

> Let me give something!—though my spring be done,
> Give to the children, ere their summertime!
> Though stirred with grief, like rain let fall my rhyme
> And tell of one whose aim was much: of one
> Whose strife was this, that in his thought should be
> Some power of wind, some drenching of the sea,
> Some drift of stars across a darkling coast,
> Imagination, insight, memory, awe,
> And dear New England nature first and last,—
> Whose end was high, whose work was well-begun:

Of one who from his window looked and saw
His little hemlocks in the morning sun,
And while he gazed, into his heart almost
The peace that passeth understanding, passed.

In the final sonnet he signals the approach of death and sum-
marizes what he can leave as nothing more than "perhaps a
monument of labour lost." If this is all that he can give, he
asks God, "Who givest all things," to make a living testimony
of his whole life—a tree "struck scarlet by the lightning, utterly/
To its last limb and twig"; a tree "red-ripened to the heart:
shedding its leaves/And autumn sadness on the dim spring day."

The image of the lightning-struck tree which first appears
at the start of the memorial to Anna and which reappears in the
final sonnet is a fitting symbol of Tuckerman's entire life. Like
this scarlet tree, he has endured the fury of the power that has
transformed his life into one huge red scar of grief. Yet both
he and the tree endure. Each in its own way remains productive,
giving all it can as a sign of its will to live. Such strong will
which refuses to accept defeat is sure indication that hope and
fortitude can banish thought of a meaningless life and can
provide peace to a trouble-scarred one. The optimism that
grows as the sonnets unfold and the poet's assertion that he
has mastered his perplexing troubles are good witnesses that
his poetry is a testimonial of a life well lived.

Quite late in his life, Tuckerman regrouped all his intellectual and spiritual forces to add an epilogue to his poetic
autobiography. This poem, *The Cricket*, is proof of his ultimate
certainty of happiness arising from a worth in life and a rejection of death without meaning. At the heart of this poem are
Keats's ideas that "The poetry of earth is never dead" and that
"The poetry of earth is ceasing never."[7] The winter song of the
cricket is a pledge of the perpetuation of nature's work because
it continues the summer song of the grasshopper. This romantic
view bears witness to his triumph over dark doubts, uncer-
tainties, and despair. His lonely ways, his innate brooding and
discontent were intensified and prolonged by the tragedy of
Anna's death. Yet, the stubbornness to overcome such obstacles
leaves the clear impression of a strong character worthy of the
grand New England tradition which nurtured it.

IV   *The Disturbing Solitude*

"But I add crag to crag"

Tuckerman stood aloof from the mainstream of social and political activity that flowed through New England. His temperament did not allow him to engage in prolonged indignation when Greenfield was changing and his favorite haunts were being overrun by railroad tracks and Irish shanties. Rather than raise a loud but futile voice like Thoreau, or shout like Wordsworth, "Is there no nook of English ground secure/From rash assault?"[8] Tuckerman preferred to go away to find a fairer spot. As science began to burgeon and to introduce new ideas, he was content to know that it has limitations and boundaries and that ultimately the astronomer would have to turn from his telescope with which he scanned the vastness of the skies to examine his own soul. Man, whatever he could attain or whatever he had been, was ultimately a child of nature and must ever return to her.

The Civil War, which produced such a spate of martial verse, is little noticed in Tuckerman's poetry. Sonnets VI and VII in Part IV deal directly with the quiet sorrow of an old man looking for a letter from the boy who had drawn "the blind lot of battle." The letter never arrives, but still the old man waits, "silent, and with the fiery eye of grief." Another is the eulogy, "G. D. W." Still another work relating to war is "An Incident," written about 1872. A commentary on the post-bellum period rather than on the war directly, it is a dialogue between an English expatriate who sees America falling apart and unable to live up to its promise of greatness and Tuckerman, who is sure that his country will rally from its low condition to unite, to prosper, and to fulfill its great democratic destiny. The ode written for the dedication of the soldiers' monument in Greenfield may be added to this short list of his "war poems."[9]

To escape from a hostile environment, to turn the back to petty events, to withdraw from society in general were easy to accomplish. But to divorce himself from the dominant ideas of the day was practically impossible. His insistence to live his life as independently as had the experimenters at Brook Farm, at Fruitlands, or at Walden arose from a self-centered disposition. He noted the small events and the great ones, but he willingly let them pass. Why should he busy himself with what he had no hand in creating or with what he had no power to control? It was pertinent enough for him to try to make sense out of his own life, to rid himself of the brooding and melancholic ways that nagged him. In his grief over the death of his wife and in his attempts to find inner peace and understanding, he had sufficient reasons to live in a disturbing solitude.

While Tuckerman's circumscribed world kept him from active participation in the large issues of his day, it did not prevent him from being in tune with the spirit of his age. The intellectual milieu of New England strongly shaped his thought as well as his poetry. A fugitive from the Brahmin tradition, he could never completely shake off its influence; as a result, his poetry is always dignified, genteel, and decorous—even when his emotional disturbance is at its height. Of great importance is his ready acceptance of the spirit of Transcendentalism, which suffused his thought and equated his mental outlook with that of Emerson.

Although Emersonian ideas abound in his work, it would be a mistake to think of Tuckerman as a disciple. He is Emersonian in much the same way as are Jones Very and Emily Dickinson. All three New Englanders, living in tight worlds of their own creation and writing about their lives there, were not isolated from the strong intellectual currents from Boston that flowed to Salem, to Amherst, and to Greenfield. From time to time Jones Very circulated among the leading figures around Boston; Emily Dickinson stayed home and permitted the intellectual spirit to come into her Amherst garden; Tuckerman took the Transcendental ethic with him and withdrew to the high ground of the Poet's Seat in Greenfield.

Transcendental thought as expounded by Emerson is easily detected in their poetry; but they were still very independent, individualistic writers. What they had to say came out of personal experience and what they achieved was all their own. Yvor Winters makes the point that Jones Very speaks with the authority of experience but that Emerson often writes without authority because he "never experienced that which he recommended."[10] In writing about Emily Dickinson, George F. Whicher expresses the same basic idea:

The implication that Emerson created a point of view which other writers adopted is simply untrue. The resemblances that may be noted in Emerson, Parker, Thoreau, Emily Dickinson and several other New England authors were due to the fact that all were responsive to the spirit of the time. . . . If we now think of Emerson as the center and soul of the transcendental movement, it is not because he invented Transcendentalism, but because in his writings the new philosophy reached a consummate fruition and received its widest applications.[11]

The same position pertains to Tuckerman.

There are many examples of Tuckerman's thought which appear to be echoes of the public voice of Emerson. Emerson writes, "Build therefore your own world. As fast as you conform your life to the pure idea in your mind, that will unfold its great proportions. A correspondent revolution in things will attend the influx of the spirit."[12] He seems in this passage to be providing a general blueprint for Tuckerman's world in Greenfield. The Emersonian "independence of solitude" is well expressed in Sonnet I, Part I; the gospel of "do your work," in Sonnets I and II, Part II. Tuckerman's entire corpus of sonnets seems to be an answer and confirmation of the validity of Emerson's remark: "In this pleasing contrite wood-life which God allows me, let me record day by day my honest thought without prospect or retrospect, and, I cannot doubt, it will be found symmetrical, though I mean it not and see it not. My book should smell of pines and resound with the hum of insects."[13]

When Emerson delivered his lecture "The Transcendentalist" in Boston in the winter of 1841-42, he must have had in mind a man like Tuckerman, whose life is almost a copy of the portrait of the Idealist. Emerson's assurance that "all things will go well" if but "the soul be erect" is at the heart of the last sonnets in Part V; but Tuckerman had to win this thought after a long and difficult struggle. The Emersonian observation that beauty is evanescent and that, when one goes "forth to find it," it is gone,—"only a mirage as you look from the windows of diligence"—is caught in Sonnet I, Part III.[14]

Sometimes the ideas from Emerson's works tend to become even stronger and point to a possible direct poetic influence. For example, the phrase, "The stars of the dead calices of flowers," appears to be the firm base for "The starry flower, the flower-like stars that fade."[15] In the same sonnet, the lines "His hand, who touched the sod with showers of gold,/Stippled Orion on the midnight blue," approach closely Emerson's question, ". . . what difference does it make, whether Orion is up there in heaven, or some god paints the image in the firmament of the soul?"[16] As Emerson says, "the poet conforms things to his thoughts"; and Tuckerman's remarkable use of imagery supplies proof of the veracity of this statement.[17] "A man's power to connect his thought with its proper symbol, and so to utter it" is embedded in Tuckerman's concern with language and in his efforts to invest words with fresh meaning.[18]

The essential principles and dicta which Emerson espoused are central to Tuckerman's intellectual outlook and make him a Transcendentalist. He was not like Emerson, universal in his scope; he excluded from his world political, economic, and social problems and may therefore be considered provincial. But a fuller and more accurate description is that Tuckerman was a Transcendentalist and a fiercely independent individual. Thus, he used the Emersonian ideas as vehicles to carry him along the lonely road leading to a place where he could divest himself of the perplexities which engulfed him, where he could triumph over grief and isolation and prove to himself that he could lead a restful life in an essentially restless era.

CHAPTER 3

The Poet's Art and Craft:
'The myriad meaning of a word'

I *Making of Sonnets*

"Though stirred with grief, like rain let fall my rhyme
And tell of one whose aim was much."

THE EXCELLENCE of the sonnets so overshadows the conventional poems that there is great temptation to consider the latter as apprentice pieces and the former the result of such apprenticeship. But, since the subject matter makes it clear that the writing of both types occurred concurrently, the works cannot be chronologically divided into earlier and later. Aside from some verse so obviously jejune that it must be relegated to an early period when Tuckerman was a trifler, his work can be readily divided in another way. The conventional poems are descriptions of events or of emotions remembered in times of Wordsworthian tranquillity; the sonnets are immediate, instantaneous records of his private life. The lyrics and the narratives are recollections of experience; the sonnets *are* the experience. In his own mind Tuckerman kept these two aspects in separate compartments. When he chose to record what had eluded immediacy or what did not require it, he treated the material conventionally; when he had to seize the fleeting moment, he adopted the sonnet form.

On the basis of the conventional pieces, Tuckerman deserves scant recognition despite the excellence of a few poems and of some passages. In the sonnets he is a true poet. The disparity in quality between the two types may be accounted for in part by his temperament. His retiring nature demanded privacy; and, when he spoke to himself and for himself, he was comfortable and confident; but, when he wrote narratives and about past experience, he was aware of being overheard and was unsure. Yet, to consider him a poet with a public and with a private voice is to oversimplify in trying to determine or to understand this sharp cleavage in his work. His voice is almost always private, quiet, and sedate in the exploration of feeling; it is loudest in the narratives, but even here the tone is so intimate that he is talking just loudly enough to be heard by a few people. But Tuckerman is a private poet who found in the sonnet a form admirably suited to his genius and his needs, one which he so mastered that he could confidently experiment with its mechanics without destroying its essential nature and character. Since it is as a sonneteer that he merits and demands attention, it is necessary to consider his sonnets in detail to appreciate his great achievement.

In their form the sonnets are like cresting waves running to the shore. Waves never break exactly at the same distance. Their crests vary in size and in shape; their running foam creates ever shifting patterns which move across the top of the waters. When they finally reach shore, they make still newer patterns darkening on the sand. Yet in their great variety, there always remains the general image of the breaking waves— each unique, each beautiful. Like them, his sonnets are true to their basic form; and, though few maintain traditional structure, they are still sonnets just as surely as the waves are waves.

His deviation from traditional writing of sonnets was consonant with his restless and tumultuous heart and mind. The stability of the fixed sonnet in the hands of Bryant and Longfellow was in tune with their temperaments, but it would have been a negation of a lifelong devotion to self-sufficiency and independence for Tuckerman to have clung to a rigid poetic form. Part of his great strength lies in his ability to alter the form to accommodate it to his needs but not to distort it beyond recognition. He knew how much power he could exert to remold the form and, by so doing, was able to exhibit its pliant but strong nature which could yield to pressure but would never relinquish its character. In his own way he proved the resilience of the sonnet form, infused it with a new vigor, and revealed its tremendous possibilities for poetic expression.

To talk about his use of rhyme-schemes is to talk about the non-existent. Very often he commences a sonnet with *a b b a*; but, after that, he deviates into whatever pattern his need seems to call for. But, while he eschewed rhyme-schemes, he was acutely aware of the power of expression inherent in the manipulation of rhyme. He gave very serious thought to this part of his work, as may be noted in his workbooks. For example, on one page, he wrote along the margin thirteen words of exact rhyme—*survey, play, sway, decay, defray, gray, ray, weigh, flay, stray, they, play,* and *prey;* and, on the other margin, he inscribed inexact almost dissonant rhymes—*barges, largess; beauty, sooty; prophet, Tophet.* More preoccupation with the latter kind of rhyming appears elsewhere in his workbooks. He put down for possible later use *"wiseacre* and *Issachar; buffet as* and *covetous; more-fit* and *forfeit; clumsy* and *Tecumseh; threaten* and *eaten; précis* and *denary."* Some of these pairs eventually found their way into his verse; but, more importantly, they indicate his concern with experimentation so that he could free himself from any possible fetters to exact expression.

Even his method of composition implies his having rhyme uppermost in his mind as a sonnet began to grow. In the early stages of what was to become Sonnet VII, Part III, he first composed two versions of the last four lines; and then, in the right-hand margin of the page, he wrote a string of words whose rhyming pattern suggests that each was meant to be the final word of each of the preceding ten lines, as yet apparently still unwritten.[1] He listed: *high, find, mind, reply, some, vain, behind, come, underlie,* and *again.* Another example is evident in his preliminary working out of Sonnet VIII, Part III. In this case he had composed the first line and left blank the next five except for the last word of each line. Here he was still undecided about the rhyme because crossed-out words stand alongside others which he had substituted. After the five endings (*less, bless, three, forth, below*), he wrote the octet.[2] These two examples illustrate his great concern with rhyme in the creation of a sonnet.

He meant for the rhyme to be an active force. When he wanted to convey a feeling of certitude or confidence, he employed exact Popean rhyme. Sonnet XXVIII, Part I, is Tuckerman's conviction that nature must be subservient to the will of God; the sure assertion is carried by steady, orthodox rhyming: *mind, find, behind, wind; abyss, amiss, bliss, this; sod, God; plead, speed; word, bird.* For an agitated mood, he used a combination of standard and aberrant rhymes to intensify this feeling. Such use of rhyme is clearly illustrated in Sonnet

III, Part II. In it the perfectly sharp rhyming of *deep, weep, keep,* and *steep* suggests stability; but, in contrast, variations on a single vowel sound emphasize the tumult and tragedy in the heart of a man who looks from a height to see his home ablaze. *Foam* and *home* modulate into *doom* and *room* and then into *come.* Another example of careful use of variant rhyme is Sonnet IX, Part IV. He expertly handles the same vowel sound as in Sonnet III, Part II; but, since the mood is more tranquil, the variations are less marked. Sensitivity to subtle sound effects is heard in this rhyming: *root, fruit, wood, solitude, hoot, shoot,* and *mood.*[3] This deliberate deviation from conventional rhyme may have been irritating to nineteenth-century ears accustomed to the more regular one of the heroic couplet. Tuckerman was moving closer to Emerson's use of it and then reaching beyond for the ultimate effect by experimenting to impart exactly the tenor of the sonnet for which he strove. Rhyme, an essential ingredient which served as an agent to create the mood or tone of the sonnet, appears superficially to be rough and untutored; but it is well calculated and shrewdly controlled.

The same situation is evident in his maneuvering of the division of the sonnet sections. In about one third of them, he adhered to the traditional separation of octet and sestet; but, in the remainder, he permitted each sonnet to achieve its own particular division. A great part of his success as a sonneteer comes from his intuitive sensing of the point of separation. The shifting adds to variety and interest; organic growth is the norm. With no fixed pattern to control or perhaps to stultify the form, he was able to build a variety of shapes and contours generally not found in restricted, standard construction. The separation may occur anywhere in the sonnet. For example, Sonnet XXI, Part II divides naturally at the end of the ninth line; Sonnet IV, Part III, at the end of the seventh line; and Sonnet VI, Part IV, has no break at all because its full impact is not felt until it rushes into the next one.

Part of the reason behind Tuckerman's surface caprice in structuring the separation arises from his desire to create surprise. His devices are unusual imagery or, more often, rare allusions. Occasionally he opens a sonnet with a startling line; but, most of the time, he withholds his intent until the very end. But the controlling image or allusion is at all times completely integrated into the sonnet and never becomes an element injected simply for its surprise or novelty. The second and third sonnets of Part V demonstrate his technique of saving the image for the final lines to firmly fix their tone. In Sonnet II he creates a mood of nature's revealing herself in half-lights and dim shapes, but the vagueness is swept away in the surprisingly beautiful natural image in these final lines: "As the night-heron wading in the swamp/Lights up the pools with her phosphoric breast."[4]

In Sonnet III the mood is one of mystery of nature felt "when summer-daylight dies." He senses the great varieties of life that abound untarnished by any knowledge of the enigma of nature that envelops them. In the last two lines the mystery is sharply and suddenly focused on the poet's "little boy, symbolling eternity,/Like the god Brahma, with his toe in his mouth." Sonnet VIII, Part V, is the most evocative example of this technique. In it he describes a bucolic view. The language is simple, clear, and unexciting for thirteen lines, and then the last line marvelously and explosively illuminates the garden lodge and its surroundings:

> The low-built cottage buried in the vale,
> Wooded and over-wooded, bushed about
> With holm tree, ople tree, and sycamine.

Such artistic endings endow the sonnets with unsuspected energy, with a strangeness unencountered in the works of any other American sonneteer.

II *Use of Rare Allusions*

"A dim old page"

To careful planning of the rhyme, to internal separations, and to brilliant final imagery must be added a fourth element which helps make these sonnets so remarkable: allusion. At first sight, Tuckerman's use of allusion lends an air of obscurity; instead of achieving surprise, it creates temporary bafflement. This condition is brought about by his insistence on using for his allusive material the names and the places almost lost in the darkest corners of antiquity, history, and mythology. The obscurity is sometimes compounded by his altering an already historically dusty name to gain a more appealing sound or to integrate it more closely into the sonnet. These allusions are so far from the usual poetic stock of historical and mythological figures encountered in other poems of the day that they suggest that Tuckerman had populated a private world with imaginary people who lived with him in the woodlands and fields around Greenfield. But such is not the case; there is no privately peopled land in Tuckerman's imagination and there is no secret mythology.[5]

The identification of allusions leads to a greater appreciation of his artistic perception; they are always an organic part of the sonnet and never mere ornament. How effectively he uses a single allusion to penetrate every line and to assert its total control of a sonnet's tone and substance may be noted in Sonnet XXXVII, Part II (Eponina). It is based on the tragic story of Sabrinus and his wife, Epinone, in the days of the Emperor Vespasian. When Sabrinus was defeated in an uprising against Vespasian, he escaped, burned his house to the ground, and caused the circulation of a story that he had perished in the conflagration. He then went into hiding in a nearby cave. When Epinone heard the rumor of his death, she vowed to die by starvation. Moved by her devotion, Sabrinus had her brought to the cave, where they lived for nine years. On the rare occasions when she ventured among the villagers, she always played the role of the tearful widow. During this long period she bore twin sons but was forced to keep them secret. Eventually, Vespasian's soldiers unearthed the family, and Sabrinus was condemned to death. Epinone pleaded for her husband's life; and, although Vespasian was at first moved by her pleas, events of that time forced him to carry out the order. Not wishing to survive, Epinone insulted the emperor and she, too, was killed. According to one tradition the twins were spared.[6]

In adopting this story Tuckerman used an alternate ending in which Epinone begged Vespasian to save her children but her efforts were useless and they, too, were slain. Tuckerman chose the very moment when she is bringing her children from the cave for the first time in their lives in the hope that their presence might help soften Vespasian's heart. Such careful choice of this specific incident sharpens the focus on the allusion and prepares the reader to link Epinone's tragedy with his. His poems are like her children in that both are offspring born in sorrow and kept in darkness; at this moment, the children

and the sonnets are just emerging from the dark into their first
glimpses of the light. As Epinone begs Vespasian's pardon, so
Tuckerman hopes his words will find favor in God's "pardoning
love." The idea of the children's being "buried" in the cave for
nine years easily and naturally associates itself with the sonnets'
being "buried" for a long time; and, together, these associations
blend into the central thought of his wife, Anna's, being
"buried" too.

The allusion is the foundation of this sonnet. The opening line
is startling because of its abrupt introduction of the relatively
unknown Eponina. Her name has been changed slightly by
shifting of vowels, probably to create a softer sound. Tuckerman, who is honest with the reader, immediately reveals her
identity in some detail; he tells of

> Eponina brought, to move the king
> In the old day, her children of the tomb
> Begotten and brought forth in charnel gloom,
> To plead a father's cause,

and then alludes to himself by adding,

> . . . so I too bring
> Unto thy feet, my Maker, tearfully,
> These offspring of my sorrow, hidden long
> And scarcely able to abide the light.

After making this parallel, he joins his plea with hers:

> May their deep cry, inaudible, come to thee
> Clear through the cloud of words, the sobs of song,
> And sharper than that other's pierce thine ears—

and then in a single line concentrates upon his own "thought,
aim, utterance, dark or bright." The rest of the sonnet reunites
their sorrow. The liaison is established by the key words
pardoning and *buried*, as he prays that his words

> May find thy pardoning love more blest than she
> Who joyful passed with them to death and night,
> With whom she had been buried nine long years!

The sonnet begins with Eponina and ends with her, but she
is so intertwined with his own plight that his personal feeling
is delicately balanced against the sadness of the old historical

event; each sheds light upon the other and the sonnet becomes a beacon shining on the darkness in their hearts.

The opening sonnet of Part III illustrates the same basic approach to the effective use of a single allusion, but identity in this case is withheld until the very last words of the final line. This Dagoraus Whear sonnet reverses the technique in mode, not in principle. By keeping the allusion somewhat shrouded, Tuckerman creates what may be considered willful obscurity but actually it is not so. As the sonnet progresses, a series of strong clues points to recognition of the allusion.

Dagoraus Whear is Degory Wheare (1573-1647), appointed first professor of modern history at Oxford on October 16, 1622.[7] His lone great work is a Latin dissertation, *De Ratione et Methoda Legendi Historias*, delivered at Oxford in 1623. It was once so well known that Edmund Bohun's translation, *Method and Order of Reading Histories*, went through three editions—1692, 1698, and 1710. Tuckerman chose this obscure professor because his name suggests a sense of weariness and because his book is long forgotten. Wheare and his book become the core of the sonnet designed to re-create the poet's own feeling of utter dullness on a dreary day. As he lingers over the tome, a sudden ray of sunshine falls on the page and a bird begins to sing. He quits the library; but, by the time he gets out of doors, the sun and the bird are gone. Disappointed, he returns to the book's dreary pages. The alteration of Degory to Dagoraus and the dropping of the final letter in Wheare enhance the languid atmosphere of the sonnet; the long drawn-out vowels capture the sense of a spiritless, lazy afternoon. At the same time, *Dagoraus* permits a mild pun on *dagger*; such a book kills the day and numbs the spirit.

As in the Eponina sonnet, Tuckerman very early presents solid details about his allusive character. He says,

> I sat perusing a forgotten sage
> And turning hopelessly a dim old page
> Of history, long disused and out of date,
> Reading 'his Method' till I lost my own.

These lines tell much of Degory Wheare and even identify the translation. To identify the allusion, Tuckerman brings the sonnet to its perfect denouement: "I turned again and, entering with a groan,/Sat darkly down to Dagoraus Whear." In the

Eponina and the Dagoraus Whear sonnets, he used allusions which permitted him to say much more than their surface meanings indicate. In the former, he shows that history can repeat itself in meting out human misery; his sorrow is essentially no different from that of Eponina's. In the latter, he points out that, by transforming history into a dessicated thing, the scholar has killed the living spirit; history, reduced to a "Method," is only a dim old page that is unable to endure one sudden burst of sunshine.

The technical device in Sonnet IX, Part IV, demonstrates again the same treatment of an allusion. This sonnet moves evenly and quietly while the poet complains mildly that factories, schools, forges, and railroads are infesting the woodlands so that he is forced to search for new places of solitude. The situation is disturbing; and, like the Indians, he looks for "strange plants to medicine" his mood. Although he does not find the palliative, he feels secure when he thinks of "sagamore George." This allusion, at the end of the sonnet, lends an air of bafflement because identity is not even partially revealed. It appears too vague to suggest easy clarification; it is too private, and only those quite close to Tuckerman's life would recognize the reference. "Sagamore George" is Colonel George D. Wells of Greenfield, as was previously stated, with whom Tuckerman used to wander in the woods and for whom he had such great admiration that he called him "River-God."[8] When the white man encroached on the Indians' domain, they had to search for newer grounds; when industry invaded the woods, "sagamore George" and the poet had to do the same. Like the Indians, they moved with "quick savage sense," with "patient eye," and with "as safe a foot." The irony of identical situations is withheld until the very end, where the unifying agent is "sagamore George." Sagamore is a New England Indian chief; George, the civilized white man. By combining both into a brilliantly cohesive epithet, Tuckerman has paid a compliment to his close friend, has recognized the plight of the Indians, and has successfully used the allusion to drive home his point.

Sonnet XII, Part V, follows the same pattern. In it he explores the idea of death as a means of uniting him permanently with Anna. He compares their hoped-for reunion with the mythological tale of the swift and tragic deaths of Phadimus and Tantalus whose story is found in Ovid's *Metamorphoses*.[9] The luckless pair were wrestling playfully after a day's work when an arrow pierced them as they stood breast to breast. They groaned and fell together.

In the opening lines, Tuckerman intimates that the sonnet will deal with a Classical myth but holds back all further reference to it until the last line. He describes how valiantly he and Anna strove to stay together by ignoring social forces which tried to separate them: "The countless hands that push true hearts apart" were as ineffective as "The clouded looks of hate, the harrowing eyes." Yet, their lives were shattered by the mysterious power of "the bitter god of love," who, "As in revenge for some disparagement," "pierced and pinned" them together with an arrow. And with this same arrow they "fell, like Phadimus and Tantalus." The allusion illuminates the existence of incomprehensible forces which, even as they bind, separate and which work so indiscriminatingly that human understanding cannot fathom the reason for the paradox. The myth performs its function ideally by illustrating the universality of the theme and by demonstrating man's inability to be master of his own fate.

In the Eponina, the Dagoraus Whear, the sagamore George, and the Phadimus-Tantalus sonnets Tuckerman used in each a clear, strong allusion to fortify a single, definite personal experience. Each allusion possesses sufficient strength to carry its burden. To have used more than one would have cluttered the sonnet; to have distributed the load would have weakened the allusive force and destroyed the sharp focus. However, when Tuckerman undertakes to consider a very general idea which needs as much support as possible, he brings to bear on the subject as many allusions he can muster. Sonnet XXIV, Part I, is an outstanding example of this strategy. The theme is that, when man is faced with doubt, he can often find truth revealed in a dream or in a vision. In the opening lines he states his thesis clearly: "yet surely truth has beamed/Oft from the gate of dreams upon the brain." He then asks why doubters resist this possibility so vehemently. The final four lines present a gallery of five women whose strength of vision defied mere reason:

> Did Manoah's wife doubt ere she showed to him
> The angel standing in the golden grain?
> Had Deborah fear? Or was that vision vain
> That Actia, Arlotte, and Mandané dreamed?

At first these lines appear overbold; the crowding of names appears as a defect, or even as poetic abuse. A secondary reaction is that of bafflement at the allusions themselves; but, when their identities are uncovered, they become essential and powerful supports to the general idea. There is neither abuse nor bafflement. The intellectual burden demands massive support and, if the allusions are beyond ready reference or outside ordinary boundaries of familiarity, they are no less valuable; they serve their function well.

Manoah's wife and Deborah are, of course, biblical women of great vision. When the angel told Manoah's wife that she would bear a son, she never doubted: "The woman bare a son, and called his name Samson: and the child grew, and the Lord blessed him" (Judges, 13.24, 25.). Deborah showed great strength by believing in the vision that Israel would not be vanquished; her faith was not misplaced (Judges, 4.5.). She was called the "great dame of Lapidoth" by Tennyson; she was the *mulier splendorum*.

Actia is Actaea in Ovid's *Metamorphoses*, but more commonly she is known as Orithyia.[10] Actia apparently seemed more euphonious and more adaptable for the sonnet. Her place among women of vision rests in the story of her ordeal with Boreas. The terror-stricken Orithyia was enveloped in his cloak, carried off into the skies, raped, and abandoned in a savage northern country. The rape resulted in the birth of twin sons, Coleus and Zetes. She was able to overcome the great hardship of rearing them far from Athens because she was sustained by her faith that they would become great men. When they grew to manhood, they joined the Argonauts and were on the first ship that sought the Golden Fleece.

The identity of Arlotte is quite obscure. The allusion is to Charlotte, daughter of Charles IV of Spain and of Marie-Louise de Parme.[11] Arlotte is a coinage made by dropping the initial "Ch." The alteration produces a name that has the aura of antiquity and, at the same time, a sound that blends well with Actia. Charlotte was the wife of Jean de Portugal (1775-1830). In 1806 she left him because she had a vision that their son, Dom Miguel, would one day rebel against the power of his own father and depose him. She encouraged her son, but the conspiracy failed and she was shut up in a convent.

The fifth personage in the collection is Mandané,[12] whose

exact identity is in doubt. According to a story told by Herodotus, she was the mother of Cyrus; another story, recorded by
Ctesias, says that she was not his mother but his wife. Regard-
less of the conflicting stories, Tuckerman chose her as an example of a woman of great vision. Herodotus declared that she
was a Median princess who, it was prophesied, would bear a
child who would inherit the whole world. She believed in the
vision, and the history of Cyrus's triumphs attests to her faith.

By bringing together such disparate characters who had one
salient quality in common, Tuckerman assembled historical
and mythological witnesses to the power of a vision; and, by
massing them into a few lines, he accomplished masterful poetic
compression. Thus, what begins in bewilderment ends in clarity;
what appears as a poetic flaw changes into vigorous poetry.

Although Tuckerman's allusions range far and wide, from the
Indian chieftain, Wassahoale, to the Haemonian maid, their
greatest concentration is in the Scriptures. For example, Sonnet
XIX, Part I, depends for its full impact upon acceptance of
the idea that what a man performs can be judged only by God.
To put man's work in proper perspective, he ends with lines
reminiscent of God's talking to Job:

> And what canst thou, to whom no hands belong
> To hasten by one hour the morning's birth
> Or stay one planet at his circle hung,
> In the great flight of stars across the earth?

Sonnet XXXVI, Part II, is dedicated to his certainty of union
with Anna, when both will win eternal serenity. Most appropriately he adopts the confident tone of the twenty-third Psalm
and closes the sonnet with these lines:

> . . . the perfect day
> Of restoration, when in fields divine,
> And walking as of old, thy hand in mine,
> By the still waters we may softly stray!

A good deal of his life's struggle and his personal inner victory
is contained in the biblically inspired lines: ". . . into his heart
almost/The peace that passeth understanding, passed."

Sonnet XV, Part III, is a declaration of faith in God. There
is more to life than continual striving to make a mark at the

expense of divine guidance. The heart of this sonnet is a re-working of "I am the resurrection, and the life: he that believeth in me, though he were dead, yet shall he live" (John, 11.25.). Tuckerman transforms this passage into: "I am the Truth, the Life too and the Way," and comments, "It stands, a word to comfort and appal,/A summons grave and sweet, a warning stark." How powerfully he felt the impact of the Scriptures may be realized by the fact that he chose to carve on Anna's grave-stone lines from Lamentations of Jeremiah, 1.12, but he altered them slightly by inserting after "Behold and see" the phrase "all ye that pass by."

In addition to the use of the Scriptures in the sonnets, atten-tion needs to be given to some jottings in his workbook. On one page he had written six specific references so placed that each pair formed a unit with contrasting elements. For example, he wrote "Meribah, ex. 17, 7" and "Admah, Deut. 29, 23." Meribah is the location of the rock which brought forth water when touched by the wand of Moses; Admah, an infamous place like Sodom and Gomorrah. A second pair has "Merodach, Kings 2, 20" beside "Eutychus, Acts 20, 9." The association here combines the unfortunate ruler and the unlucky boy who fell asleep during one of Paul's long sermons, toppled from the third loft, and was taken for dead. The third jotting brings together "Achan fell in Achov" (Joshua, 7.) and "Gamaliel" (Acts, 5.). The contrast in this case is between those who took the law into their own hands and stoned the thief, Achan, and those who listened to Gamaliel, the great doctor of the law, who urged the high priests not to kill their prisoners for having preached against them. At the heart of this contrast is the admonition from Peter that it is right to obey God rather than men. Achan disobeyed the word of God and was stoned to death; the apostles obeyed and were spared. Although these notations were never incor-porated into his work, they afford an opportunity to see the use of biblical references in what may have been preliminary stages in creating the nucleus of a poem.

Tuckerman was aware that allusions in general and biblical ones in particular could be spoiled by overuse. He makes his point very clear in "Lines Written in Blue Ridge, Virginia," a posthumous work. Here he depicts an ignorant Irishman who referred constantly to the Bible but knew nothing of it. The jamming of allusion and reference into a few lines produces chaos born of stupidity. This Irishman could most learnedly talk upon

> The doers and the deeds in one
> Epistles and Apostles;
> O'er Scriptural names of Achsah, Ruth,
> And Leah would hitch and hirple,
> To Lydia, faithful to the truth,
> A seller too of purple.

And in the next stanza the confusion is multiplied:

> Nicaula in her robes of state,
> Dorcas, Demetrius, Lilias,
> And men of might, the scarceknown great
> From Gilpin back to Gillias.

Tuckerman's allusions are confined to relatively unknown persons and characters, but they are no less real than more famous ones. The important thing is that they are used successfully. For some readers they may be less attractive than more easily recognizable ones, but their newness and strangeness create an exotic background which sets the sonnets apart from the conventional poetry of his contemporaries.

Allusions which appear to create a private mythology are matched by place-names which very often suggest a private geography. Tuckerman uses these names in much the same way that he uses allusions. The first requisite is that the place be the proper background against which the sonnet can achieve its maximum effect; the second, that the place-name be real and identifiable in the poem. Some references are patently clear and need little or no explication. For example, in Sonnet V, Part III, he refers to "the Common" and there is never any doubt that the reference is to the Boston Common. He mentions the pond, the burial place near the corner of Tremont and Boylston streets, and his own boyhood home nearby. He illustrates that a familiar place can be changed into a fearful one in the minds of children.

In Sonnet XI, Part II, Whately Woods, located just south of Greenfield, is the familiar, close background which intensifies the actions of the weary engineer who is deceived by "the witch-light of the reedy river-shore," even though he is traveling a well-known road. In Sonnet XVIII, Part II, the Indian spelling, Quonecktacut, for Connecticut, helps to sustain the atmosphere of the woods when the Indians roamed them freely. The image of "thunderous purple like Cascadnac peak" in Sonnet V, Part II, is less clear. *Cascadnac* is an invention derived from Cascade and *nac* or *nock* and means a lone mountain peak in the high Cascade Range.

An elaborate use of place-names occurs in the sequence comprising the Long Island episode. His main purpose is to suggest that his visits there were journeys like those of Bunyan's Pilgrim. To accomplish his aim, he sets the episode in a region where villages bear such quaint names as "Fire Place," "Devil's Neck," "Mount Sinai," and "Good Ground." These places hardly sound real, but the only variation is the translation of "Belle Terre" to "Good Ground." The sequence ends with reactions to the story he had heard. The tale had aroused his boyish imagination, which wandered to strange and distant lands. In his active mind, he looks at the varying shapes of waves—one looks like Gibraltar and another like "the grim Rock of Visgrade." By mentioning this vague place, he points out just how far a child's fancy can roam. Visgrade is a variant of Visegrád. In central Hungary, a town by that name was dominated by a high rock upon which a prison and fortress had existed from the year 1000 to 1300. This remote and forbidding site is well described by the lone adjective *grim*.

Sometimes Tuckerman's knowledge of geography is inexact, but the occasional lapse is not a serious impediment to locating the reference. For example, in Sonnet VIII, Part IV, he mentions "those vast weeds that off d'Acunha's isle/Wash with the surf and flap their mighty fronds." D'Acunha's isle is Tristan da Cunha in the South Atlantic, but the Sargasso Sea, identified with the weeds and fronds, is far to the north.

An effective and subtle use of a single place-name is found in Sonnets VIII, IX, and X, Part V. In this trio Tuckerman's basic idea is that the presence of beauty transforms the commonplace and that beauty has a natural home from which she should not be removed because, when uprooted, she can never be transplanted. The first sonnet describes a remote, romantic place. The poet recalls "A garden lodge, shut in with quaintest growth,/A slender girl with still kine pasturing near." He brings the scene to a closer view.

The little valley hidden in the pine,
The low-built cottage buried in the vale,
Wooded and over-wooded, bushed about
With holm tree, ople tree, and sycamine.

The diction divorces this scene from New England. When describing a dwelling in western Massachusetts, as in Sonnets XV and XVI, Part II, he speaks of the typical red farmhouse with its black roof, a path lined with feverfew, all set in a clearing. But here the farmhouse is a "garden lodge," a "low-built cottage" half-buried in "quaintest growth": "holm tree, ople tree, and sycamine." The variations on farmhouse and the strangeness of the growths provide an air of distance and enchantment. In the second sonnet, the atmosphere is sustained as the "slender girl" becomes a symbol of beauty and her presence enriches ordinary things by "Touching all objects with transfiguring power." He presents a list of commonplace objects upon which beauty has cast her spell: "The housedog at the door, the village school,/The village in the hills, the hills of Ule." The third sonnet asserts that "Better wild roses died their natural death/Than evilly or idly them to rend." But in the last five lines the illusion of a mysterious place is shattered by a most homely image:

Tight as a stem of grass within its sheath,
You yet may draw and nibble, touch the sweet
With the tip tongue and browse the tender end
Half-vacantly; but not to be put back,
Or swallowed in, but sputtered from the lip.

This image appears to be disturbing and at odds with the tone of the previous sonnets, but the shock of jarring juxtaposition wears off at once when it is realized that Tuckerman has inveigled the reader into a small world of romance which, in fact, never existed. All the elements which created a vague, dreamy place are real and consistent with his general poetic practice. And in the dazzling line, "holm tree, ople tree, and sycamine," the trees are not inventions despite their overtones suggesting "home," "opal," and "sycamore." The holm tree is the common evergreen oak of Europe; the ople, an obsolete name for the ordinary witch-hazel; the sycamine, a variant of sycamore and found in the Scriptures.[13]

In the middle of the second sonnet, the place is clearly named as "Ule." It appears to be an imaginary village, derived from the last syllable of *Ultima Thule,* the mythical northernmost habitable region. Such an obvious conclusion is unwarranted. In all Tuckerman's work place-names are actual, and this one is no exception. He has gone to considerable effort to describe the place and firmly establish its existence. The garden lodge and the slender girl may be located in the village of Ula in southeast Norway. Lippincott's *Gazetteer* (1952) states that Ula is a summer resort village at the foot of some high hills. Tuckerman mentions "village" twice and lays heavy emphasis on the hills. He locates the village in a northern region by referring to "long moonlight nights." This place is far enough from New England to have a romantic air, yet not so far as to be outlandish; his contemporaries would not have thought a village in a Scandinavian country excessively remote in view of their interest in that part of Europe. It may be recalled that Belle Terre and Visegrád, mentioned in other sonnets, are also summer resorts.

Once Ule is recognized as a real site, these three sonnets assume a much richer quality than they would have had the name been a romantic invention. The reality of Ule strengthens the symbol of beauty, and the whole subject is linked to a reality which makes the central theme active and concrete. The absolute necessity that Ule be a real place is borne out in the extended image in the last five lines of Sonnet X. By moving from the supposedly dreamy atmosphere of Sonnet VIII into the reality of Sonnet IX, the poet is preparing the way for the very familiar image to insinuate itself gracefully and forcefully at the end of the sequence. Thus, the image which seems so out of place in a nebulous setting is clearly a studied one to make the point that all three sonnets merge into actuality and that, while the idea being considered may be discussed without a habitation, its effectiveness is increased by its being rooted in a very specific spot.

Tuckerman's handling of allusive material is so consistent throughout his poems that any idea of a private world vanishes under close scrutiny. Intriguing as an imaginary world may be, the real one increases poetic intensity and, more importantly, brushes away fogginess which might blur a sharp focus. Tuckerman's great care in embedding identifying hints and concrete details frees him from any imputation of practicing literary deceit or of barricading himself from reality by erecting an impenetrable wall which the reader can never fully breach. His world is remote but always real and ever accessible. The irony is that Tuckerman, the dreamer who shunned most of society to live privately, is ultimately a realist. He has no Xanadu, no Auber, no Poictesme; he has for his province the whole universe, both in time and in space. By roaming at will from Long Island to d'Acunha's isle, from the Poet's Rock in Greenfield to the Rock of Visgrade in Hungary, he has mapped out territories left unexplored by more timid writers who chose to follow well-traveled highways.

III Use of Imagery

"The laws that gird the globe"

Tuckerman confesses that in his thoughts there were "Some power of wind, some drenching of the sea,/Some drift of stars across a darkling coast."[14] The wind, the sea, and the stars perform important functions in the sonnets. Generally they move beyond the range of mere simile to become symbols. The wind is always a disturbing and saddening influence; the sea is the harbinger of fear and its constant motion represents the conflict of an unsettled state of mind; the stars that drift across a few sonnets are guides of hope and symbols of stability.

The power of the wind makes itself felt insistently and brings with it a steady, consistent note of sadness. Tuckerman feels "the dark wind strain" and often finds himself "entangled in the night,—a night/Of wind and voices." He hears the "wind's low surge"; he feels its presence in a deserted house when the "sunset wind/Sighs in the chambers . . . Or shakes the pane." It sometimes has an "icy breath"; at others, it is "ominous"; but invariably it is his implacable enemy. He vents his fury on the gale:

> Oh, might I on the gale my sorrow fling!
> But sweep, sweep on, wild blast! Who bids thee stay?
> Across the stormy headlands shriek and sing
> And, earlier than the daytime, bring the day
> To pouring eyes, half-quenched with watery sight,
> And breaking hearts that hate the morning light![15]

The wind is closely connected with deep anguish. He roars "to the unmoved skies;/But the wild tempest carries away" his cries. It directs his thoughts to Anna's grave. "I look on the sweeping corn and the surging rye,/And with every gust of wind my heart goes by!"[16]

Although the wind exerts a strong influence, the sea makes an even greater impact. Salt spray, waves, and storms create a force which produces deep fear. When he talks about his being "Apart from friends, remote in misery," he couches his feelings in an image of the sea. He is like a man who walks and "weeps by alien brine," like a marooned sailor who "looks sadly seaward at the day's decline." In a pensive mood in Sonnet XXV, Part I, he writes: "Or sad, I look/On miles of moonlit brine, with many a bed/Of wave-weed heaving." The same use of the sea-laden weeds may be found in Sonnet VIII, Part IV, where the inability to separate good from evil is compared to "those vast weeds that off d'Acunha's isle/Wash with the surf and flap their mighty fronds/Mournfully to the dipping of the wave." The sea maintains its portentous character in Sonnet X, Part III, in which his spirit is eroded by the same breaking waves which form caverns in the bases of high rocks by the sea. The keynote is struck at the very start: "Sometimes I walk where the deep water dips/Against the land." He views the sea and the ships "With joyless heart." Restless as the sea, he hears only his own moaning and "the wailing of the wheeling plover." He compares himself to

> . . . this high rock beneath whose base the sea
> Has wormed long caverns, like my tears in me:
> And hard like this I stand, and beaten and blind.

The sea often appears in his thoughts of Anna, as in Sonnets XXI and XXII, Part II. In the first, he pictures a "dim bark" carrying her away; but, as he looked across the sea and "yearned to follow," he realized that for that one moment he had lost "the old fear of the sea." Yet it remains the symbol of sorrow, for he says:

> I on the jetty stood and watched the ship,
> The wave broke fresher, flinging on my lip
> Some drops of salt. I shuddered, and turned away.

The second of these sonnets, XXII, continues the image as he hopes that Anna has found "Some shore of rest beyond the labouring wave." The whole view of the sea as an unstable, unreliable, fearful force is exposed in Sonnet XIV, Part II. He stands with Anna on a "neck of sand" watching bathers at their "shuddering play," aware of the "trembling turf" and the "drenching of the wave." He recalls a day with her when the sky was "standing like eternity" in contrast to "white feet flying from the surging surf/And simmering suds of the sea!"

The unpredictable, disturbing ways of the wind and the sea as natural forces correlate with Tuckerman's own unsettled condition when he was overcome by grief and anguish. But, in the wonder of the movement of heavenly bodies, he finds symbols of hope and security. An astronomer in his own right, Tuckerman knew and understood the advances that were being made and valued such scientific knowledge. But science was inadequate to explain the majestic, awesome working in the heavens. In Sonnet IV, Part V, he explores the heavens and concludes that scientists, great as their worth may be, fall short of total appreciation of the wonders of the firmament. The scientist

> Sees all the worlds in utmost space withdrawn
> In shape and structure like a honeycomb,
> Locates his sun and grasps the universe
> Or to their bearings bids the orbs disperse;

he may even seem to "stand like that great angel girt/With moon and stars." The emphasis is on *seem* because man can never replace God. The identity of the great angel "girt/With moon and stars" is in Psalms 8.3,4:

> When I consider thy heavens, the work of thy fingers, the moon and the stars, which thou hast ordained;
> What is man, that thou art mindful of him? and the son of man, that thou visitest him?

This symbol of stability is meticulously worked out in Sonnet XVII, Part II, when Tuckerman considers the movement of Mercury, Mars, Earth, and the moon in their ordered motion in relation to his disordered grief. There are natural limits to everything:

> Roll on, sad world! Not Mercury or Mars
> Could swifter speed or slower round the sun
> Than in this year of variance thou hast done
> For me.

He finds serenity in the sense of natural order as

> The moon runs round and round; the slow earth dips,
> True to her poise, and lifts; the planet-stars
> Roll and return from circle to ellipse.

Just as the total aspect of the heavenly bodies serves symbolically, so do its various parts. Sunlight is associated with life and leisure in Sonnet XI, Part I; the fading sun is cause for sadness in Sonnet V, Part I; and a single ray of sunshine is enough to chase away the gloom in the Dagoraus Whear sonnet. While the sun is a symbol of solace, that of the moon is allied to beauty's "transfiguring power." The "Ule" sonnets capture this view: "All the long moonlight nights I dreamed of Ule/And in the dark half of the months my heart was there." The sky itself is a symbol of immutability. In Sonnet II, Part II, his own restless ways are contrasted with those of the farm boy who sleeps "whilst overhead/Creation moveth." And in Sonnet XIV, Part II, the ceaseless motion of the sea is balanced against the "hard and blue" sky.

The stars are especially dear to him. He hears them "tick audibly" and describes a smile that "like starlight gleamed." He believes that a knowledge of the stars is a valuable part of education. In Sonnet VI, Part IV, the old man teaches the boy history, myths, and mathematics; but beyond that he shows him Job's Coffin, the Golden Yard, "the nine moonstars in the moonless blue," and the "great Circle of the Bestiary." Such homely references give the stars a warmth and friendliness that the purely scientific names cannot. Job's Coffin is the constellation Delphinus (The Dolphin); the Golden Yard is the belt of Orion; the nine moonstars form an apparently dim celestial grouping best seen on a moonless night; and the Bestiary is, of course, the Zodiac.[17] As a result of such knowledge, the boy grows up to "love the sky."

The stars are symbols of hope. The despair of "the doomed sailor, left alone to die," is eased when he looks up at

> The dewy stars of home,—sees Regulus shine
> With a hot flicker through the murky damp
> And setting Sirius twitch and twinge like a lamp.[18]

In Sonnet XXIII, Part II, a glimpse of a renewal of hope is felt when the inaccessible "great asterisms" are seen "Low in the sky, like frosty Sirius,/To snap and sparkle through the winter's night."

The "power of wind," the "drenching of the sea" and the "drift of stars" are only parts of his thoughts: "Imagination, insight, memory, awe,/And dear New England nature first and last"[19] were always in his mind. "New England nature first and last" infuses and pervades the sonnets with vigor, with a new view of rural New England, and with an unmatched surge of poetic enthusiasm. It is the most potent and effective source of energy which exerts influence over Tuckerman's sonnets.

As has been noted, nature was the center of Tuckerman's life from his earliest days. When a schoolboy, he preferred the fields and woods to the classroom and books; when a "pilgrim" in Canada or on Long Island, he so absorbed the splendor of nature that in adult moments of recollection the sound of the sea and the flight of the bird were still vivid. Even his quitting Boston for Greenfield was decided in part by his love of nature. Therefore, it is not surprising that, when he started to write verse, New England's flora and fauna were everywhere in evidence as his work took shape. His attitude toward nature was never that of an idling, romantic dilettante; he was a serious student of botany who looked with a clear eye at the flowers, the plants, and the trees. His observation is always acute and accurate, and he knows exactly what he is observing. He seldom talks vaguely about birds, insects, flowers, and plants; he gives them specific names and provides details to supply utmost clarity.

In his earliest work he was so overwhelmed by the profusion of nature that he was unable to cope adequately with it. Quite often he would insert lists of plants and flowers just for the sake of the sound of their names, or for no apparent reason at all. Other times he would draw an elaborate picture of a bird or a flower as an exercise in giving poetic utterance to a scientific observation. Occasionally, he would achieve a brilliant stroke by correlation of a natural image and a human action. As he improved the mastery of his art, he learned more and more how to integrate New England's nature into his poems.

In connection with his artistry in correlating nature and poetry, it is valuable to bring to mind some of Emerson's ideas. At the heart of Emerson's essay "The Poet," published in 1844, is the idea that all great works of art have an organic quality, that nature is a symbol, and that the poet ought to use pictorial and imaginative words: "Nature offers all her creatures to him as a picture-language."[20] The poet's work should be free from rigid, stale form and rhyme; it should grow and flower like things in nature. Such ideas were in Tuckerman's mind just as they were in the minds of Dickinson, Thoreau, and Whitman. More diverse writers than these are unimaginable; yet, by some strange force, all were impelled toward the same goal by vastly different roads.

Wandering about the hills, along the river's edge, or in the dank swamp, Tuckerman knew intimately every rock, every plant, every flower, every insect, every bird, and every small animal that came into his range. He took all that he saw, reduced it to its essentials, and put it into his verse. How successfully he achieved organic unity may be witnessed in many of his works.

"Nature and Necessity" has a memorable picture of a partridge. In the narrative, he tells of a "little ragged girl who ran with us" and likens her actions to those of a partridge which

> runs to guide you from her nest:
> Now buffets at your feet, now falls she down,
> Because her brood is hatched;—
> I think 'twould move a heart of stone to see,
> A heart of adamant or chalcedon,
> How pitifully she
> Wept with one eye, and with the other watch'd!

In Sonnet XXVI, Part I, he wishes to show nature's contradictions. First, he tells of belief in his divine sense in discovering nature's secrecies and thereby understanding her contradictory ways. But, to explain how widespread and vast they are, he has to admit that his own knowledge is scarcely adequate. To emphasize magnitude in her inexplainable works, he combines pictures of three New England birds to bear witness to the central idea:

> The night-hawk blew his horn at sunny noon;
> And in the rainy midnight I have heard
> The ground-sparrow's long twitter from the pine
> And the cat-bird's silver song, the wakeful bird
> That to the lighted window sings for dawn.

Another outstanding example is in "An Incident," a post-humous work and one of his very last since one manuscript is dated February 7, 1873. He states emphatically that, after the Civil War, there will come a period of peace and a rebirth of life in the desolate places where war has ravaged the land. The fiery steed of war rushes across the land; but, even as he charges, he leaves the imprints of his hooves in which little birds will make nests and life will burgeon once more:

> And where red Strife has stamp'd with angriest stride,
> Mid its own orchard-bowers again shall hide
> The cottage home with its small children, like
> The bird's nest set in the print of a horse's foot.

And, in the last two lines, he envisions in the skies a symbolic image of America's resurgence: "A single Star thro' twilight twinkling strongly/Beneath a single blood-bright Stripe of cloud!" The flight of the swan, the wheeling of the plover, the winging of the gull, and the phosphoric breast of the night-heron illuminating the pool supply still more images which exemplify Tuckerman's observations of birds.

Large animals have scant place in his sonnets. The horse, the wild deer, and the house dog are merely mentioned; but the world of tiny insects assumes importance. The bee is seen on "the maple log" and the blossoming cherry is so covered with bees that it "hummed all day in the sun, the April blue." The cricket was to Emerson a "poor, tooting, creaking" insect, but to Tuckerman it assumed much nobler proportions. In the extreme stillness of Sonnet X, Part I, he mourns a young man's death. The clouds pass softly, tiny petals drop on the shingles, and the only sound is that of the cricket as he "chides beneath the doorstep stone." In Sonnet XXX, Part II, against a desolate background of burnt forest and snowflakes "in utter solitudes," he hears "the cricket's cry" so loudly that it "appals the heart and fear takes visible shapes." These impressions of the cricket as a symbol of death and destruction are heightened by their invariably being set in quiet surroundings. In *The Cricket*, to be considered separately later, this lowly insect becomes a mighty symbol of life and death.

The butterfly and the grasshopper appear together, not in the traditional flash of color and gaiety, but in just the opposite guise. As a boy, Tuckerman hunted for "Tattered and dim the

last red butterfly,/Or the old grasshopper molasses-mouthed."
In Sonnet III, Part V, the controlling image is "A crowd of
flea-like grasshoppers, like flies/Presaging dry and dry con-
tinuance." The final sonnet of Part IV calls attention to the
"miracle" of "The worm that, touched, a twig-like semblance
takes" and "the craft that makes/The twirling spider at once
invisible."

The birds and the tiny insects move and flit through the
Berkshire woods and fields, and Tuckerman employs them
to good advantage. But his chief interest is in the plants and
the flowers; and these have most important and conspicuous
places in his poetry.

IV *Use of Native Flora*
"And dear New England nature first and last"

Tuckerman's propensity to observations of plants and flowers,
manifest in his youth, continued uninterrupted throughout his
life. All his work is a testimonial to this devotion. His grand
array and catalogue of flora found in the Berkshires is unique in
American poetry. In proportion to the number of poems he
wrote, he devoted more lines to plants and flowers than did
any other American poet. No New Englander saw them with
a more appreciative sense of detail; no contemporary used
them to greater advantage. For some, they were ornaments or
only vehicles for moral observations; for Tuckerman, they were
never uprooted for such purposes. He handled them gently
and put them into his verse with discrimination either to aug-
ment an idea or to give it picturesque and concrete qualities.

His appreciation went far beyond the visual beauties because
he combined his observations to include both the poetic and
the botanic. No detail escaped his attention; no plant or flower,
bright or dull, large or small, grand or humble, went unnoticed.
When he placed flowers, herbs, or plants in his verse, he kept a
clear eye on their sizes and colors and had a sharp ear for the
sounds of their names. The result of meticulous attention to
every floral detail embellished and enriched his poetry in a
manner unrivaled in nineteenth century American poetry.[21]

In dealing with plants and flowers he seldom used disguising
names and never inventions. Sometimes the Latin form served
his purpose; sometimes, the common one; and, occasionally,

the colloquial one. But, in every instance, selection was based on the mood of the sonnet. For example, in Sonnet IV, Part I, he mourns the passage of his youth, the vexations of sorrow, and the perplexity of a life spent "Mid unfulfilled yet unrelinquished sins." To convey its tone and mood, he compares his condition to that of the lowly Jimson weed, more commonly called the stinkweed, a rank and poisonous plant. These names would be inappropriate for the dignity inherent in the sonnet, so he turns to the Latin name, *stramony,* derived from *Stramonium.* As a result, he creates this highly charged ending: "Like purple-poison flowers of stramony,/With their dull opiate-breath and dragon-wings." The botanic detail is exact; the poetic usage, correct.

In contrast to this example, Sonnet I, Part II, deals with a comparison of his roaming in the woods with the work of a farm boy. He wonders if his seemingly idle ways are useless. To describe this humble theme, he selects the herb that most closely suggests his own mental state. Avoiding the scientific or the generic name, he uses "poke-berry." His apparent indolence is epitomized by this homely nomenclature, with its connotation of "slow-poke" and the line is not only enhanced but fortified by the unadorned and non-poetic verb, "spit." The details about the herb supply everything needed to blend herb with mood. Its roots and berries have emetic and purgative properties; the dark purple berries are very juicy. Thus, when he returns from the woodlands, his hands stained crimson, he asks, "Was it a thorn that touched the flesh, or did/The poke-berry spit purple on my hand?"

Two highly agitated sonnets filled with his grief which arises from untimely deaths afford more examples of his sensitivity and discrimination in placing flowers in his verse. In Sonnet XIV, Part I, he describes his grief for a friend whose young bride had just died. The friend

> Fell from himself and was content to weep
> For eyes love-dark, red lips, and cheeks in hues
> Not red but rose-dim, like the jacinth-flower!

The jacinth-flower, an obsolete name for the hyacinth, is outstanding for its delicate bluish-red color. As a hyacinthine flower, it carries with it a most suitable story. The hyacinth was believed to have sprung from the blood of Hyacinthus, who was accidentally slain by Apollo. The rare coloring of the flower matches the red lips and the rose-dim hues of the bride, and the sad old tale adds poignancy to the friend's grief.

In contrast to Sonnet XIV, Sonnet X, Part I, is presented in muted tones. A young man had died in "terror and anguish"; his life had been uncomplicated by deeply felt emotion. The sonnet is simplicity itself; there is no place in it for brilliant flowers or exotic plants of bright or subtle color. The black roof of the lonely house slopes toward a mountain-ash whose tiny white petals fall on the roof. The juxtaposition of the blackness of death and the whiteness of young, innocent life endows the sonnet with exact emotional quality.

The idea that beauty exists everywhere in nature is the thought expressed in Sonnet VIII, Part II. Beauty is found in the most common of flora as in the rarest and most exotic. In making his point, Tuckerman groups together three very ordinary New England flowers with rather intriguing names: mayflower, sidesaddle-flower, and whippoorwill-shoe. The slight and almost lustreless subject matter is balanced against intensely accurate descriptive elements; in fact, this sonnet is a botanical one more than a philosophical one. The mayflower is found during April, usually in pine woods; the whippoorwill-shoe is found in May in shady, dry places; the sidesaddle-flower, abundant in early June, is a swamp-plant. Their colors and shapes form a pleasing and contrasting picture. The mayflower, more generally known as trailing arbutus, is rusty brown, hugs the earth very closely, and hides itself among dried leaves. The sidesaddle-flower is green with some dark red veins and, as a member of pitcher plants, is easily seen and recognized. The whippoorwill-shoe, a member of the gaudy Orchis family, is a showy, yellowish-green flower with a white and crimson-pink bag. All this variety among well-known plants in the Berkshires is evidence that beauty is everywhere in nature. The natural habitat of these three plants is very accurately described in the sonnet. He mentions "Ransacking sward and swamp" for the sidesaddle-flower and whippoorwill-shoe; and, at the end of the sonnet, he says that the mayflower may be

> gathered equally
> On desolate hills, where scantily the pine
> Drops his dry wisps about the barren rock,
> And in the angles of the fences found.

A counterpart to this poetic lesson in botany may be seen in the detailed description of a laurel-blossom in "The School-Girl":

> So her young life,
> Above the gulf, detached, and yet detained,
> Suspended swung; as o'er a fresh-fallen pool
> A laurel-blossom, loosened by the rain,
> Hangs at its pistil-thread,—hangs, shakes, and falls.

Sonnet XIII, Part II, is a loud echo of Tuckerman's conventional poem "The Question," in which the poet permits his imagination to adorn his beloved with a profusion of rare gems and flowers. This sonnet, apparently a reworking of "The Question," is more controlled; but the lover's exuberance is undiminished when he recalls "his mistress' features hour by hour"; he is enchanted by her

> Dark eyes, dark lashes, and harmonious hair
> Caught lightly up with amaryllis flower,
> Haemanthus, eardrop, or auricula.

The catalogue of flowers suggests the rush and tumble of the lover's unbridled imagination. "Amaryllis flower" is a cliché but it gives strength to "Haemanthus," a flower in the amaryllis family, the name of which calls to mind the god of marriage and at the same time reminds the reader that *Haemanthus toxicarius* yields an arrow poison. "Eardrop" and "auricula" are well chosen; their names provide verbal alliance, but there the resemblance ends. Only in the thoughts of a mindless youth would these flowers adorn a loved one's hair. The eardrop is more commonly called lady's ear-drop and is a member of the geranium family. Orange or red-orange, it is thickly speckled with tawny-red dots. When plucked, it wilts quickly. Two of its other common names strike an ironic note: *Spotted Touch-me-not* and *Kicking Colt*. The auricula is of the primrose family, often called bear's ear on account of the shape of its leaves.

All of Tuckerman's reverence of nature is summed up in Sonnet X, Part IV, a cordial invitation to share with him his knowledge and love of her. He has brought together the worm, the spider, the barberry flower, the "singing sand by the cold coast," and the "little chick-wintergreen star." In each he sees nature's miraculous powers working in secret. He asks the reader

if he has *touched* the worm that "a twig-like semblance takes,"
if he has wondered what craft makes "The twirling spider at
once *invisible*," if he has *smelled* "the spermal odour of the
barberry flower," if he has "*tasted* the sour" of the chick-
wintergreen leaf, and if he had *heard* "the singing sand." The
senses, the strange ways of nature, and even the habits of the
smallest of creatures are important to a fuller appreciation of
"Nature's secrecies." What is more important is that Tuckerman
is anxious and willing to share his own appreciation with the
reader. Humanity and external nature join hands here in a
fine tribute to both.

The floral world of Tuckerman is as rare and delicate as it
is profuse and faintly bewildering. Weeds, herbs, plants, and
flowers take root in almost every page where they grow as
organically as if in their natural places in the fields, the woods,
the swamps, the waysides, and the hills in the Greenfield region.
He was so well equipped to take full advantage of his excellent
knowledge of the flora that he seldom needs to use a flower
more than once; but, when he does, he is likely to choose an
alternate name. The rose and the violet, so common in the
works of other poets, are not often encountered. Instead, he
uses with confidence and with good judgment such low plant
life as sorrel, knot-grass, spurge, cinquefoil, feverfew, waste
balm, pond lily, brook flags, and pearlwort. Tall majestic plants
appear with less frequency, but he does not overlook the purple
vervain spike or the mullein stalks. The ordinary elm, the
hemlock, the tamarac (better known as the larch), and the
ubiquitous transcendental pine have their places, too.

Tuckerman's use of the New England flora is as exact and
as poetically appropriate as his use of mythological, historical,
and biblical allusions; they fit into a pattern that is clearly de-
fined, albeit one intricately and cunningly wrought. This same
kind of almost finicky care extends into his use of similes. But
here he reverses the trend and turns from the strange to the
homeliest of objects to achieve his striking effects. The material
for his figures consists of the most familiar of things, a familiarity
which seems to destroy their poetic usefulness. Yet he injects
freshness into these humble, simple things. He holds his belief
"like a blade"; he pores over the landscape "like a book"; he
stands "like a fire-hardened trunk"; he sees the celestial universe
resembling "a honeycomb." He was able to make his words

take on many forms, like the stream from an ordinary garden hose which "Now spouted rainbows to the silent skies,/Now kept it flat and raked the walks and shrubs."[22] A sick man regains sense of his surroundings by feeling "like a wreck that has outlived the gale," and sounds return to him like "the faint rustling of the watch beneath his pillow." He hears a clock that "ticks like a belated foot" and notes "the twanging of the hours."

Sound as a device to project mood is evident in these examples: "Grow green in your gray shadows/And greener than the season grows the grass." The utter quietness of Sonnet X, Part I, is emphasized by the sibilants in its closing lines:

> Where the black shingles slope to meet the boughs
> And—shattered on the roof like smallest snows—
> The tiny petals of the mountain-ash.

The sh of the final word is almost a command to be silent. The noise of Sonnet XII, Part I, is furnished by clank and clashed; the sound of wind is heard in "waves and washes in the windy blue." The brittleness of his fancy is sharpened in these crisp lines: "As snapping from the brands a single spark/ Splits in a spray of sparkles ere it fall."

Tuckerman's concentration on turn of phrase and balance of epithet produces memorable lines and passages. For example, in Sonnet VII, Part I, "The bread of tears becomes the bread of life" is a carefully balanced line with the varied meanings of "bread" providing artistic compression and, simultaneously, binding tears to life. In the same sonnet, the line, "wasted red has wasted to white away," describes dead leaves under a pine tree. The movement from a live, red leaf to a dead, white one is carried in the dual meaning inherent in repetition of "wasted." The red leaf is "wasted" because its beauty is no longer a living part of nature; the white leaf is the result of the former's having "wasted away."

An ingenious use of a colloquial phrase to give it new meaning is in the Phadimus-Tantalus sonnet, where the pivotal force is in " 'Twas one to us." In its ordinary sense, this phrase is used in the poem to point to petty, gossipy people who have tried to separate the lovers and to show that all their arguments have been met with complete indifference. At the same time, it assumes a rich and new sense because it refers to the unity arising out of the legend of Phadimus and Tantalus. A more involved example is in these lines in Sonnet III, Part IV: "That pace it round all day and never sleep,/That watch the wall all night and pace it round." Here, Death is a watchman who never rests. The lines are balanced syntactically to convey the idea of the relentlessness of Death. By placing "That pace it round" at the beginning of the first line and by repeating it at the end of the second, Tuckerman achieves a circular motion to underline his picture that Death makes his inexorable rounds as he watches from a high tower. The vigilance of Death's watch is further emphasized by ending the first line with "never sleep," by starting the next with "That watch the wall," and by balancing "all day" against "all night" in the middle of these two lines. In Sonnet XVII, Part II, exact choice of verbs not only describes the movement of the moon, the earth, and the other planets but also delineates their relative speeds in the solar system. Thus, the moon "runs round and round"; the slower earth "dips/True to her poise, and lifts"; the planets "roll and return from circle to ellipse."

Metrical deviations which tend to create the impression of a crude and careless poet are, on the contrary, very deliberately designed. A lingering and slow sunset is contained in a line which drags itself as far as it can go until it can offer no more and eventually must break and sink because of its length. Appropriately, the line comes at the end of the sonnet, and it fades away reluctantly, like the sun: "Dim fades and, as the sun fades, fading likewise dim." The truncated line, "And simmering suds of the sea," is as short as it can possibly be to suggest the span of life of a wave. On the other hand, the stability and long life of the sky is expressed in a regular, orthodox line: "The blue loft standing like eternity."

The mechanics involved in proper placing of sequences within each sonnet series is done shrewdly to give additional power and thrust. Chronological ordering and thematic linkage are inevitable but are not the only ones. A way to gain maximum effect is to arrange sequences in such order that each reflects light upon the other. A good example is in the lofty, inspiring ending of Sonnet V, Part IV: "And the dear fellow aid of man to man." This idea is carried over into the next sonnet as the old man helps educate the boy, and it also moves into Sonnet VII in which the high-sounding phrase becomes a mere slogan. The

Civil War has destroyed its validity and has made a mockery of it when the farmer realizes that the boy had been killed in battle.

Another example is in the comparative treatment of themes in Sonnets XXIII and XXIV, Part II. The former deals with "the great asterisms [that] mount and burn/In inaccessible glory"; the latter, with the most familiar of objects, "The house, the grove,/The street, the face, the ware in the window." By setting down the extremes of the sources of human knowledge, Tuckerman has laid great stress on the basic theme that neither source reveals truth. The endings of Sonnets XV and XVI, Part I, demonstrate how a single image, that of the tears and the cup, gains in power by extension. The first of these two sonnets ends with the utter helplessness of the grief-stricken lover:

> He kissed her hands, her mouth, her hair, her head,
> Gathered her close and closer to drink up
> The odour of her beauty, then in tears
> As for a world, gave from his lips the cup!

There is anguish enough here, but it tends toward the maudlin. However, this initial impression fades in the light of the final lines of the second sonnet. Fiery intensity results from recurrence of the image:

> And now he breathes apart, to daily drink
> In tears the bitter ashes of his love,
> Yet precious-rich and a diviner draught
> Than Agria or Artemisia drank!

The tears in one sonnet become the solvent for the "diviner draught" and make possible "bitter ashes." In this way *tears* is divested of its traditional, hackneyed use.

By such ordering of entire sonnets, Tuckerman treats them in much the same way that he does words, phrases, images, allusions, and references. He thinks of the individual sonnet as a part of the whole and even of each sequence, while a self-sufficient unit, as functioning within the larger scope of the series. All these technical and mechanical devices work toward the achievement of a unified, integrated art form.

The materials for the poems are not substitutes for the poems themselves. All of Tuckerman's skill in using artistic devices and ingenuity in executing good judgment do not in themselves

guarantee successful achievements. What informs the five
sonnet series is his deep and steady concentration on the main
purpose—to examine and to explain to his own satisfaction
his inner life so that he may try to reach a fuller understanding
of its meaning. His ability to pursue relentlessly self-observa-
tion with objectivity and his integrity in describing and in
evaluating his feelings produce the cohesive ingredient which
binds all the separate elements into an artistic entity. The parts
may be admired; his skill in handling them appreciated; but,
ultimately, his force of poetic intention and its fulfillment must
be recognized. Tuckerman's personal victory over dark doubts,
fears, and grief stands as a symbol of the success of his sonnet
series to gain for him another victory as an incomparable
sonneteer.

CHAPTER 4

The Cricket: 'The Shadow grows'

I *The Theme*

"Might I but find thy knowledge in thy song!"

TUCKERMAN'S BEST single work, *The Cricket*[1] is a dream piece in which the poet, adrift in time and place, reviews his life that has been so objectively and minutely observed in the sonnets. A mature work, *The Cricket* is marked by a quietly confident tone, by a relaxed and tension-free atmosphere, and by a long, retrospective point of view in contrast with the petulance, indecision, fear, and doubt that pervade the sonnets. A good deal of the success of the sonnets is accounted for by the use of a private voice so suitable to the subject matter; much of the success of *The Cricket* is due to Tuckerman's ability to adopt a new and public voice. In some of the sonnets the reader barely overhears the poet as he mutters to himself, but in *The Cricket* the reader is confronted with a voice pitched to a larger audience.

Essentially, it is a happy poem in which freedom and escape from the external world are achieved by complete surrender to forces that Tuckerman had hitherto been unable to understand or to conquer.[2] *The Cricket* is a capitulation made willingly and almost eagerly and joyfully because through it he has brought peace and comfort to a mind that had experienced a lifetime of troubles, that had retaliated against these troubles, and that had wrested little victory from invincible adversaries. The battles of his life are at last finished, and *The Cricket* is testimony of his relief and contentment at the outcome.

The subject of this poem is Tuckerman's assessment of his life with special reference to the meaning of life and death as parts of his existence. In the sonnets he had satisfied himself that death is an experience which leads to a better and greater life than the earthly one, and in this poem he maintains this idea. However, he designed *The Cricket* to be at once an objective view of life and death as well as a fusion of his own life with these abstractions.

The cricket was not a capricious choice; it is a creature in nature very closely associated with Tuckerman's retiring personality and with his withdrawn way of living. The cricket is mentioned only twice in the sonnets: in one instance, its voice foreshadows death; in the other, it comments on grief. Out of the quietness surrounding death in Sonnet X, Part I, "The cricket chides beneath the doorstep stone"; out of the recollections of youthful days spent "In utter solitudes" in Sonnet XXX, Part II, "the cricket's cry/Appals the heart and fear takes visible shapes."

It appears more frequently in other poems. In "The Stranger" it brings somber tidings at the precise moment when summer has gone "but ere Autumn's cold/Bade the fall-cricket cease his mournful hymn."[3] In "The Old Beggar" it carries a sad message:

> . . . when the daylight is weary to see,
> When the grasshopper's song shall a burthen be,
> When the jar of the cricket is bitter to hear,
> And the hum of the harvest-fly stings the ear.[4]

The cricket appears disdainful of petty human behavior; for, while people are busy with trifles, "in the fields of faded grass,/ The cricket ticks and twitters."[5] At other times it is a harbinger of cheerful sounds. In "Mark Atherton" the jingling of gold is "like the innumerable chink and chime/Of the night-crickets hidden in the grass";[6] in "The School-Girl" is heard "the ceaseless chime/Of insect-voices singing in the grass."[7] In "Under the Locust Blossoms," its voice is pleasantly welcome and induces repose:

> I waited for the night
> Till the crickets tinkled drowsy
> In their beds of clover white.
> Or fell silent at my footfall, one by one.

Tuckerman transforms this simple, tiny creature into a complicated and universal symbol when he combines its various and contradictory alliances with sorrow, with happiness, and especially with dreaming. The fact that the poem is a dream does not rob it of solid construction and design, of clarity, and of vigor; the dream is clearly seen; there is nothing nebulous about it.

In construction *The Cricket* is an irregular ode in five sections with iambic lines of varying lengths and with fairly orthodox rhyming. The first, a brief invocation of eleven lines, sets the friendly, quiet, and restful mood which is the necessary preparation for the dream. The diction is simple, almost colloquial; the syntax is orderly, never strained; the tone is dominated by activity barely seen, faintly audible. The "humming bee purrs softly o'er his flower"; the "dogday locust singeth in the sun"; the cricket's voice is "Muffled and lost in bottom grass, or loud/By pale and picket." Here the cricket's voice is so varied that it suggests both the bright song of life and the muffled sound of death. The scene is a vague place, with "lawn and thicket," "bottom grass," and "pale and picket."

This section ends on a cheerful note: "Shall I not take to help me in my song/A little cooing cricket?" This modest, tranquil opening is followed by a section of twenty-seven lines which are an invitation to the reader to join the poet on a lazy afternoon in partaking of the luxury of resting under a tree by a brook or in a shady bower and to "mark [the] minstrel's carol." The invitation is made in rich language to contrast with the simplicity of the first section.

All the elements of nature conspire to produce a condition to induce sleep. The background for this sleepy afternoon is more gaudy than that of the first section, but it is still rather vague. The wind flutters; sounds "mingle and meet/Murmur and mix"; there is a garden bower "Trellised and trammeled with deep drapery/Of hanging green." The brook mutters and moans to itself as it moves along; the sky is "swooning-blue." While the cricket sings quietly, the poet and the reader succumb to the "dead fragrance" of the "poppy's dark refreshing flower," which beats on the temples and stuns the "sense to slumber." As they sleep through the afternoon, the cricket pipes its song; and, as evening approaches, the song grows louder and louder; the whole landscape has become alive with crickets—"Rising and falling like the sea,/Acres of cricks!"

The third section describes a dream that begins with the poet's childhood and quickly encompasses his entire life. In the first four lines, the happy days of youth are recaptured. The cricket that had fallen silent as the boy neared resumes his

chirping "with vibrance crisp and shrill" as it sits "in the sunshine to rejoice!" This happy glimpse shifts abruptly to a darker
one: the dreamer has forgotten the pleasant image of youth
and the cricket's daytime song. Now it has become a "Night-
lover too; bringer of all things dark,/And rest and silence."
This view aligns itself with the early adult life of the poet; the
cricket's cry brings to mind his old fear of the sea. Its night voice
is disturbing because it brings "Always that burthen of the unresting sea/The moaning cliffs, the low rocks blackly stark."

These dark and hostile remembrances become so firmly fixed
in the dream that the familiar field changes into a "long flat
seaside beach," the cricket is like "the wild seamew," and the
poet imagines that his unsettled mind is like "the overturning
wave."[8] The turbulence of the sea and all its disquieting associations now yield to thoughts of death. This aspect of the
dream is a recollection of loved ones who have died. The
cricket's song brings "lost accents from the grave"; the poet
is "dreaming of those who dream no more of him." In his
mind there appears to be a jumble of "heyday looks and
laughter come again;/Forms that in happy sunshine lie and
leap." As those who have died pass through his mind and leave
"partitions deep," he is probably dreaming of his wife, of his
son, of Colonel Wells, and of others; for these are transformed
into a "crowning vacancy." The section ends with thoughts
of Anna when hearts were "wild with love and wo/Closed eyes,
and kisses that would not let go."

This dream of only twenty-four lines is a kaleidoscopic review that touches quickly but effectively on the three salient
parts of his life that were discussed in great detail in the sonnets.
At the same time there is revelation with astonishing clarity of
how, in the unguarded moments of a dream, he confesses reten-
tion of fear of the sea and grief for Anna, even though he had
stated in the sonnets that these haunting troubles had been overcome. Once again, the background is uncertain—as it should
be, perhaps, in a dream in which the cricket's song is the controlling element.

In the fourth section, the dream moves back to ancient
times. The subject has become the glory and the celebration
of the lowly cricket as he is transformed from a member of
"the insect crowd" and from a messenger of life and death into
a universal creature symbolizing the sorrow that has afflicted

all mankind. Gods and heroes have listened to the cricket's chime in "that old graceful time/When Greece was fair." The cricket is no longer in plain bottom grass but is "Softly astir/Where the long grasses fringed Caÿster's lip"[9] or "where/Reedy Eurotas ran." These ancient, almost forgotten streams, contrasted with the familiar brook, are romantic places "with glimmering sails of swan and ship." The cricket leaves these to join mythological characters. It becomes associated with Xenaphyle's "tender flute," with Psammathe's grief, and with Pan's death.

The unhappy tale of Psammathe in the dream episode provides an insight into the deepest recesses of Tuckerman's mind; the story is replete with overtones which recall his poetry and his sorrows. Briefly, Psammathe, fearing her father's wrath, exposed her infant Linus, whom she had borne to Apollo. When the child was torn to pieces by dogs, Psammathe's grief was so intense that it revealed her as the mother. The songs of mourning for Linus became an annual rite, and Psammathe's dirges became the well-known Linus songs.[10] In the province of dreams there may be a place for disconnected thought and illogical order. Perhaps Linus is Tuckerman's poetry; and Psammathe, the poet. Or Psammathe may be a confused image of his grief for Anna; and Linus, a tormented vision of his son, Edward, who had died so young.

The reeds along the Eurotas, the soft sounds of the flute and the mournful songs of Psammathe readily bring to mind the death of Pan. Like Tuckerman and like the cricket, Pan was most at home in the woodlands, in the thickets, and in the fields where he played his sweetest tunes. In Arcady, where Pan was born, his death is signaled by loud wailing to the accompaniment of horns; but in the woods, the cricket is so overcome that his grief is best expressed in silence: "Or wert thou mute/Grieving for Pan amid the alders there?" If Pan's pipings can symbolize poetry, poetry's death means the end of the eternal song of the cricket. This silent grief establishes the point that, without poetry and without the cricket's song of life and death, Tuckerman's own world is, indeed, "*pan*ic-stirred." Such a thought is enough to turn into a nightmare the dream that had started quietly and pleasantly.

The fifth section starts as a continuation of the dream sequence. The first ten lines search for the meaning of the cricket's song. The answer may be found by the Enchanter who had touched the leaf "So that articulate voices now he hears/In cry of beast or bird or insect's hum." Through magic, the dreamer may be successful in his quest and become the cricket's "true interpreter." The blending of the cricket and the dreamer into a close relationship ends the dream, and they are united for the rest of the poem. If the poet were sure of what the cricket's cry really meant, he would "stir/The world to hark" and then would be satisfied with life's meaning and would be content to bring the cricket's wisdom to the world, "Content to gain at last some low applause/Now low, now lost." Even if its song remains a mystery, the poet will still admire it:

> Then cricket sing thy song, or answer mine
> Thine whispers blame, but mine has naught but praises
> It matters not.

The final ten lines reflect a reconciliatory attitude dominated by a sense of the inevitability that soon "The Shadow grows,/ The moments take hold of eternity." With this observation, the poet urges the cricket to rejoice even though the unheeding world swings on "Unmoved by Cricket-song of thee or me."

II *The Technique*

"Horns of Arcady"

The irregular form of *The Cricket* works against its immediate success, for it appears fractured or disconnected, since each section is a short, independent poem. But below the surface irregularity it has a strong, orderly, unified structure. When it is read as an afterpiece, as an epilogue or as a coda to the sonnets, the non-restrictive form inherent in the ode is ideal because, by its very use, Tuckerman establishes his emancipation from formal and technical problems of composition and, more importantly, announces his freedom from any sort of restraint— the thought which controls the whole poem. In the sonnets the external pressure of the form forced the subject matter into cogent shape, with theme and form vying for control. Here, the subject matter takes full charge, and the structure is subordinate. The form of *The Cricket* thereby becomes in itself a commentary on Tuckerman's new attitude.

The relative formlessness of the invocational and the invitational sections poses no problems. However, the sudden change from Section II to Section III appears too abrupt; the former is highly irregular in construction; the latter, quite orthodox. In measure, tone, and discipline, the third section is roughly a twin-sonnet of eleven and thirteen lines, respectively. The initial eleven lines have the marks of a sonnet: the first four lines are regular in length and conform to the traditional *a b b a* pattern; the next quatrain is also regular and has a *c d d c* rhyme scheme; the following two lines are a couplet; and the abbreviated sonnet-like form terminates with a truncated line, "And the overturning wave." The first line of the second part of the twin-sonnet is linked to the eleventh line by rhyme, with the remaining twelve lines in quite regular couplets.

Deviation from the pattern set in the first and second sections is logical and necessary. The regularity in the third section slows the tempo and sets the mood for the dream. But more importantly, the sonnet-like construction is suited to the subject. In this section Tuckerman is dealing with the same personal themes of the sonnet series and, therefore, a poetic structure akin to that of the sonnet is artistically correct if subject and form are to have a mutually harmonious relationship. But, by just avoiding two regular sonnets, Tuckerman succeeded in permitting the subject to control the form.

The relative rigidity of the third section is a good contrast to the fourth, in which the subject moves from the personal to the impersonal as the cricket resumes its place as the central theme. The excitement of the fourth section is heightened by charged language and by introduction of highly suggestive allusion. The form is like that of the second; as a result, the poem assumes its initial shaping. The fifth section retains the looser construction and the strong, romantic overtones of the preceding section. Gradually, as the poet and the cricket merge their identities, the poet's voice is heard above that of the cricket; and, as the romantic aura fades, the language becomes direct and simple as it was in the invocation. By this skilful handling of varieties of form and of diction, *The Cricket* maintains unity and completeness.

As an ode, *The Cricket* has a musical character which is fully exploited to develop further organic unity. The cricket's song is heard throughout, but other sounds are introduced to create a brilliantly conceived symphonic effect. The emphasis on *humming, murmur,* and *muffled* establishes a quiet beginning. Then there is a gradual development in "muttering and moaning," "falling water and fluttering wind," and "no few faint pipings." The sound grows "louder as the day declines"; the crescendo is increased by such phrases as "vibrance crisp and shrill," "the wild seamew," and a general stirring of activity in sound coming from the "unresting sea" and "the overturning wave." The crescendo is intensified as a new set of musical sounds are introduced: the "reedy Eurotas," the "breathings mild" of the tender flute, and the lamentations of Psammathe. The grand climax comes in the last line: "Though the lost forest wailed to horns of Arcady."

The last section is a diminuendo beginning with "cry of beast or bird or insect's hum" which is a prelude to the cricket's piercing sounds alternating with quieter ones barely heard "amid the stems and straws." These varying sounds are followed by still more tranquil ones caught in "The ceaseless simmer in the summer grass," and this quietness finally gives way to a "whisper." By this use of musical suggestion and motif, another kind of unity is created. These various artistic devices remove any doubt that this poem is carelessly built or casually planned. It is a craftily designed and a delicately executed work.

III *The Assessment*
"Escaping colour"

The Cricket is a fine achievement with ample strength and power to maintain an independent life. In it Tuckerman has displayed his genius as a true poet and has demonstrated beyond doubt his mastery over varieties of poetic utterance as well as his ability to bring together into a highly integrated union verse of simple statement (Section I), poetry of deep emotion (Section III), and of glittering, colorful imagery and allusion (Section IV). This poem makes its fullest impact, however, when placed in relationship to the sonnet series as an extension of the thoughts expressed in the concluding sequence. These final sonnets end with a wish—almost a cry—to give something to posterity and with a plea to gain at least a glimpse into an understanding of life's essential meaning. Tuckerman is desperately in need of resolution of his strife and justification for one "Whose end was high, whose work was well-begun." In the very last sonnet his resolution appears to be wavering when he thinks that his life is "Perhaps a monument of labour lost" and, at best, like "a tree/Struck scarlet by the lightning, utterly/To its last limb and twig."

The Cricket is both a clarifying statement of what Tuckerman thinks of himself and an affirmation of his conviction that his life and work are not a testament to a life spent in futility and despair. The connection that links *The Cricket* to the final sonnet is in the repetition of the image of the scarlet tree. In Sonnet XVI, Part V, it is not only lightning-struck but also dying out of season, "shedding its leaves/And autumn sadness on the dim spring day." In *The Cricket* the tree reappears with the "autumn goes" as an image of the poet's life so that when "The Shadow grows . . . Our lives are gone/Like thinnest mist,/Like yon escaping colour in the tree." The emphasis on "escaping colour" rather than on leaves shedding out of season offers an image that is in harmony with nature and with life and not one that is a sport of nature. A secondary connection is in the suggestion of life as a dream in the final sonnet, where everything appears so strange that he asks himself "had I dreamed?" *The Cricket* answers that query by asserting that life may be a dream, but if so, it is a memorable one filled with excitement and color.

These links between the sonnets and *The Cricket* indicate that Tuckerman meant the latter to be read in conjunction with the sonnets because it is his final statement on his life. The poem is unquestionably a triumphant personal conviction that even a poet whose voice is as unappreciated and undervalued as that of the cricket still has a long and enduring life. *The Cricket* asserts an unshakable belief that his poems, like the cricket's song, will endure.

CHAPTER 5

Other Poems:
'A monument of labour lost'

I *Some Lesser Works*

"Let me, though turning backward with dim eyes,
Recover from the past one golden look."

THE QUALITY of the rest of Tuckerman's poems is so uneven that only a handful are worth notice and preservation;
except for occasional fine lines and images, they may be safely
permitted to retain their present state of obscurity. Lack of consistency is normal in the works of many poets, but in the case
of Tuckerman it is especially noticeable because of the thin
corpus of his work and because of the tremendous disparity between the excellence of the sonnets and the ineptness of the
other pieces. Several can be discarded on the grounds that they
are juvenilia, apprentice work, or merely exercises in verse
making. The unsuccessful poems are generally vague, meditative
ones in which he rambles aimlessly as he is shrouded in dim
doubts and "bosom-sins" which assail him. Diffusion, lack of
direction, and awkward expression are obvious, serious flaws.
Strangely enough, these bad poems were often written at about
the same time that he was composing the sonnets; and it is
tempting to try to find a reason for the disparity in quality.
But one must not yield to a temptation in which there is nothing
except the hazard of guesswork; to linger over such speculation
is profitless. It is much more worthwhile to give some attention
to those poems which deserve a hearing and add to an appreciation of Tuckerman's work.

One of the best poems is "Under the Locust Blossoms," a late
work redolent of all the lush qualities noted in the second and
fourth sections of *The Cricket*. Shadowy, dream-like and haunt-

ing, it could have been incorporated as a sixth section of the ode. This line appears in *The Cricket*: "That thirsty tinkle in the herbage still"; and this one in "Under the Locust Blossoms": "Till the crickets tinkled drowsy."

The poem is divided into three stanzas each with seven lines of alternating rhyme in the first four lines followed by a triplet. The first stanza describes the dense clusters of white, heavily scented flowers of the honey-locust tree seen at sunset:

> Under the locust blossoms
> That hung and smelt like grapes:
> Under the honey-locust blossoms,—
> Faintly their breath escapes
> And smites my heart: though years have past, since I
> Beheld those clusters swinging silently,
> Silver racemes against that sunset sky:

The second stanza is an effort to recollect the time or the place where he had seen the blossoms. Vaguely, he remembers a night scene in which crickets softly chirped, but he cannot recall the exact place:

> A sky all over rosy,—
> I waited for the night
> Till the crickets tinkled drowsy
> In their beds of clover white.
> Or fell silent at my footfall, one by one.
> Did I wait? did I wander there alone?
> Under shadow, in that garden not my own?

In the third stanza he attempts to reconstruct the circumstances surrounding the experience but cannot; all that remains is the scent of the flowers:

> 'Tis but a shade of odour,
> A recollected breath,
> And I stand, a dark intruder
> The swaying flowers beneath,
> Alone, and peering on thro' anxious gloom:
> For a motion, for a glimmer, did it come?
> Oh that moment! Oh that breath of locust bloom!

While Tuckerman was writing sonnets about the death of his wife, he was composing other poems on the same subject. "Coralie" is an unsuccessful effort to express his grief, but it

is followed by an untitled short piece worthy of notice. In this
work of four stanzas, each with four unrhymed lines, he presents
a domestic scene in which he and his daughter, Anna, grieve
at their loss. The poem gains its great strength from directness
of language, from simplicity of statement, and from stable syn-
tactical construction. Each stanza is a clear, direct statement
of one aspect of his sadness. In the first, his broken heart is
compared to a rose whose heart has fallen out:

> I took from its glass a flower,
> To lay on her grave with dull accusing tears;
> But the heart of the flower fell out as I handled the rose,
> And my heart is shattered, and soon will wither away.

In the second, rain, wind, and shadows match his dark mood:

> I watch the changing shadows,
> And the patch of windy sunshine upon the hill,
> And the long blue woods; and a grief no tongue can tell,
> Breaks at my eyes in drops of bitter rain.

The third stanza introduces the domestic element and relieves
the poem of the self-centered atmosphere of the first two. He
recalls Anna when she was pushing the baby carriage while he
was at home waiting for her:

> I hear her baby-wagon,
> And the little wheels go over my heart:
> Oh! when will the light of the darkened house return?
> Oh! when will she come who made the hills so fair?[1]

The final stanza is a picture of the poet and his daughter, sad
and desolate:

> I sit by the parlour-window
> When twilight darkens, and winds get cold without;
> But the blessed feet no more come up the walk,
> And my little girl and I cry softly together.

Even though much of his work is personal, his children
seldom appear. In Sonnet III, Part V, he mentions his "little
boy"; in Sonnet XV, Part V, he refers to his children in a
general way. The only specific reference to his daughter appears
in the untitled piece.

"Margites," looked on with favor by Tuckerman's contemporaries, is an assessment of the poet's seemingly idle ways and

is a statement of futility. It is made up of thirteen stanzas, each with four lines in alternating rhyme. Although it is marred by some unevenness of expression, occasional awkward construction, and archaisms, it still retains enough vigor to be included among his better poems. The opening statement is direct and orderly:

> I neither plough the field, nor sow,
>   Nor hold the spade, nor drive the cart,
> Nor spread the heap, nor hill nor hoe,
>   To keep the barren land in heart.

So, too, is the closing:

> I walk, unknowing where or why;
>   Or idly lie beneath the pine,
> And bite the dry brown threads, and lie
>   And think a life well-lost is mine.

The poem is studded with sharply-defined images:

> But, leaning from my window, chief
>   I mark the Autumn's mellow signs,—
> The frosty air, the yellow leaf,
>   The ladder leaning on the vines.

> The maple from his brood of boughs
>   Puts northward out a reddening limb.

"Margites" was written when Tuckerman was a bachelor—before he had experienced "embraces strange,/Nor honey-mouth of lawful love."

An extraordinary transformation of tone takes place when he writes of his courtship. The quiet uneasiness of "Margites" gives way to the force of exuberance brought about by love, which is given joyful expression in "The Question," a fairly long poem of one hundred and nine lines divided irregularly into five sections. Although Tuckerman's contemporaries overlooked this poem, Walter Prichard Eaton quoted ten lines from it and Witter Bynner was enthusiastic enough to reprint it in its entirety in the preface to the sonnets as an outstanding example of excellent verse.[2] In this most pleasant piece brimming with the exotic and the colorful, one reads of "a robe/Of the Persian lilach stain,/Purple, dim with filigrane"; of a "river riding o'er/

Pearl, and priceless marbles bright,—/Onyx, myrrhine, marcasite,/And jasper green!" But occasional self-conscious, over-elaborate lines indicate a loss of control, as in the following snatch:

> Jewels crossed with jewels gleam
> On jewels, jewel-circled there;
> While, round her wrists and ankles bare,
> Gems of jewels glimpse and gaze,—
> Hyacinth, rose-stone, idocrase.[3]

"May flowers," in which the joyous theme is balanced against an even, unimpeded movement of the lines, is a simple, unpretentious poem dealing with early New England spring. The content slightly masks one of Tuckerman's basic ideas: that nature will yield her treasures and show her wonders if the searcher is patient and attentive. "Picomegan," a descriptive poem, is important not because of its intrinsic poetic merit but because its theme is fundamental to an understanding of another of Tuckerman's basic ideas: a comprehension of nature's message. He explores it first in this poem and brings it up again and again. Later he would turn to the cricket for a solution, but in this poem he listens to the sounds of the river and tries to understand its "babbling."

> But a faith thy music teaches,
>   Might I to its knowledge climb,
> Still the yearning heart beseeches
>   Truth; as when in summer time
> Through these dells I vaguely sought her,
>   In the dreamy summer time.[4]

II *A Gathering of Fine Lines*

"I spoke some soothing words"

It would be a disservice to Tuckerman to overlook the many fine lines and unusual similes which appear in the mediocre verse. In "The Clearing" two seasons are described concisely:

> The Spring wind will not come
>   Now like a pleasant rumour,
> Nor the long hot song of harvest-fly
>   To sting the ear of Summer.[5]

The month of March is perfectly seen in these lines from "A Soul that out of Nature's Deep":

> As when in many-weathered March
> May-buds break up through snow,
> And, spilt like milk, beneath the larch
> The little bluets blow.[6]

The magnificent opening of "The School-Girl" describes the evening wind rushing into the woods and then dying like a wave reaching the shore. The mild pun is perfectly executed:

> The wind, that all the day had scarcely clashed
> The cornstalks in the sun, as the sun sank,
> Came rolling up the valley like a wave,
> Broke in the beech, and washed among the pine,
> And ebbed to silence.[7]

In "Mark Atherton," small game scurry to safety when a horseman rides by:

> From his horse's hoof
> The shy frog flew; and, like a streak of light,
> The squirrel darted up the mossy bole,
> Where, glancing upward, downward, and across,
> Hammered and hung the crested popinjay.[8]

"Refrigerium," a short poem recalling Anna, has this fine passage:

> Though their very graves have run
> In the blending earth together,
> And the spider links the stones?[9]

"The fancy needs not to be new/So it be warm!" Tuckerman wrote in "Nature and Necessity." He used this dictum throughout much of his work in the form of simple, familiar, and homely images. Out of context they tend to lose some of their force, but they illustrate the application of this principle. In "The Stranger" he writes: "And open it, as I would a disused door/Locked with a dusty web."[10] In "The School-Girl" he sees

> An awkward youth in the dark angle there,
> Dangling and flapping like a maple-key
> Hung in a cobweb.[11]

The King in "Rhotruda" has a fine family but one child was destined "To vex his flesh like an ingrowing nail." In "As

Sometimes in a Grove" appears this line: "Yet to the tender tooth/The tongue still turneth." The words of Mark Atherton in the poem of that name are "smooth words, but with an edge of meaning in them,/Like a sharp acid sheathed in milk or oil." This same young man's cheek "had whitened like the winter-leaf/That flickers all day in the whistling beech." In "The Old Beggar," grief comes "home like a child to stay." Three examples occur in "Nature and Necessity": "A mitten on his tongue"; "Like flitch of bacon in a reeky flue"; and "That darkling den, rank as woodpecker's hole/With five white eggs within."

Good lines stand out clearly in the wasteland of uninspired verse. For example,

> Pathetic Autumn, and the writhled leaf
> ("Again, again, ye part in stormy grief")

> Wreck-flung, like these wave-torn beaches,
> Tear-trenched, as by winter showers.
> ("Picomegan")

> The very woods were filled with strife;
> Fierce beaks and warring wings
> Clashed in his face.
> ("A Soul that out of Nature's Deep")

> To lead thee on through dim-lit dells,
> Trembling with tiny harps and bells.
> ("The School-Girl")

> He parted fair, or, as people say,
> Went off between two days.
> ("The Stranger")

> Knitting lace like sad Rousseau
> ("Lines Written in the Blue Ridge, Virginia")

III Rhotruda—*a Narrative*

"Craftily quaint the tale"

With one exception, Tuckerman's narratives miss the mark and represent wasted energy. In "Rhotruda," the story of the Emma-Eginard episode in the days of Charlemagne, Tuckerman has changed Eginard to Eginardus and Emma to Rhotruda, the loveliest of Charlemagne's daughters. She is in love with Eginardus, the brilliant commoner in the king's entourage. One night while he was secretly visiting the princess he was trapped by a sudden snowfall, and his departure would have been betrayed by his footmarks in the snow. Rhotruda solved the problem by carrying him on her shoulders across the courtyard. The king, who accidentally observed the rare scene, realized that this was evidence of a love that went far beyond traditional courtly love and the next day permitted the commoner to wed his daughter.

This same story comprises the student's tale in Longfellow's *Tales of a Wayside Inn.* Longfellow's version is much longer than Tuckerman's because of descriptive embellishment and the introduction of several more characters; as a result, the poem loses sharp focus. Tuckerman's narrative tells the story economically by concentrating on the two young lovers. Both versions are presented in the disarming and happy attitude the tale demands, but Tuckerman has written a better poem. Not only is the episode more clearly seen but more succinctly expressed and with greater gusto. The lovers are real. Eginardus is regaling Rhotruda with tales of battle "while up the smooth white arm/His fingers slid insatiable of touch." And, when the fierce story is over, "he drew her lips to his,/And silence locked the lovers fast and long." When the princess hastens across the courtyard with Eginardus on her back, he "held his breath to lighten all his weight." When the king tells Eginardus, "Thy life is forfeit here," he quickly follows it with "but take it, thou" and turns to his daughter. He then says,

> Take even two lives for this forfeit one;
> And thy fair portress—wed her; honour God,
> Love one another, and obey the king.

In Longfellow, the king's speech is a catalogue of clichés which weaken the story and cause it to dwindle. The essential reason for Tuckerman's superiority is that he gave all his attention to the characters while Longfellow chose to concentrate on the narrative.

Among Tuckerman's papers there is one page of a letter containing an unfinished poem entitled "Poesy." This fragment was meant to be an expression of his belief that poetry will never die because it is present everywhere. It is worth preserv-

ing only as an epilogue to his full commitment to the idea that
poetry is imperishable. This pronouncement is, indeed, a confident ending for a poet who had fought so hard for his victories:

> Thou art not fled—
> Stunned by the din of this mechanic age;
> Nor chilled by wayward stress,
> Of wind and cloud to silentness;
> Nor in a poet's hermitage,
> Hidest thy gleaming head;
> Though still unwooed thy form the sight evades;
> But here amid our glens and dark blue scenery,
> And rivulets frilled with fern, and soft cascades,
> Rustling down steps of sandstone ceaselessly,
> And rocks and banks of pines,
> Thy solemn beauty wanes and shines.[12]

CHAPTER 6

Critical Commentary:
'The worth of such 'tis hard to tell'

I *Introduction*

"When critics swarm"

A SURVEY of commentaries of Tuckerman's poems is useful not only for learning to know more about this poet, but also for what is revealed about changing literary tastes from 1860 to 1965. When the privately printed edition of *Poems* was commented upon in the 1860's, the outstanding literary figures generally used regularity in form and restraint in expression—both derived from the Neo-Classical tradition of the eighteenth century—for the touchstone of acceptable poetry. What these commentators called *flaws* and *blemishes* consisted mostly in deviations from the sort of poetry written by Bryant and Longfellow. The texture of Tuckerman's sonnets was rough and therefore undesirable; the grief was too openly exposed and therefore unmannerly and anti-poetic. The poet's sharp sense of observation and his obvious love of nature were praised—but how he used them was undervalued.

Out of such commentary, it becomes clear that current literary taste had not yet caught up with the newer poetry which was emerging. Despite Emerson's long, insistent, and steady appeals for abandonment of the "courtly Muse of Europe," the established writers were still adhering to the polished and poised lines of Pope and were not in harmony with the new rhythms, the new expressions, and the new voices which were gradually silencing the traditional. The literary establishment was either unwilling or unable to accept the idea that the old, comfortable standards were tottering and, eventually, would have to make way for the newer, if uncomfortable, poetic ways. British reviewers in 1863 held positions quite similar to those of their American counterparts. At best, Tuckerman was a naturalist-poet with a sensitive feeling for natural beauty. Yet, in their opinion, this favorable characteristic could not offset his irregularity of rhyme, his discursive diction, his opacity. Like the Americans, the British were insisting on standards no longer valid in the middle years of the nineteenth century. The content of all these commentaries helps, in part, to account for the lack of early popular acceptance of the poetry of Whitman, Very, and Tuckerman and of the prose of Thoreau and of Melville's *Moby-Dick*.

When Tuckerman emerged after more than fifty years of absolute neglect, a new generation encountered his poetry. The irregularities and the other qualities which had irked and annoyed earlier critics were now considered a source of poetic strength. What had been called faults in diction, in meter, and in style became welcome signs of a break with tradition and a sure indication of a new power in American poetry. In the 1930's, when Bynner's edition of the sonnets appeared, critics looked upon the rediscovered Tuckerman as a successful experimenter rather than as an untutored mangler of poetic form. Their sympathetic approach to innovation and change, to boldness and freedom, was strongly indicative of how high a premium was now being placed upon originality.

Aside from the critic-reviewers, it is interesting to note how anthologists grappled with the problem of proper placement of Tuckerman within established categories. In one instance, he is in the group which includes Bryant, Emerson, and Longfellow; in another, he is placed alongside Dickinson and Very, as a poet of the New England renaissance. Perhaps he belongs in neither of these convenient categories. The problem has yet to be solved.

The critics of the 1950's and the 1960's, all appreciative of Tuckerman's intrinsic worth, are still trying, indirectly, to pigeonhole him by considering his work from the point of view of its intellectual content. The general questions posed are these: Is Tuckerman a disciple of Emersonian thinking? Is he a rebel, chafing at current ideas? Is he a post-Romantic much closer in practice and theory to the poets of the twentieth century? Up to now, no sure answers have been forthcoming; he is still eluding categorization.

The following record of commentaries about Tuckerman's poetry provides an added chapter to literary history, for here, as elsewhere, may be clearly seen how American literary taste had moved steadily away from Augustan conservatism; had swung in the opposite direction toward originality and freedom; and may now be veering in a new direction.

II The 1860 Edition

"The great difficulty . . . will be, to get yourself read at all"
— Hawthorne

Hawthorne, Emerson, Longfellow, Fields, and Jones Very were rather favorably impressed by the new volume; but George Ripley, Bryant, Henry T. Tuckerman, George S. Hillard, Bishop Hopkins, and Ellery Channing held mixed views. Tuckerman was such an ardent admirer of Hawthorne that, when he sent the book, he wanted it to be accepted as "an acknowledgement of deep indebtedness for very great pleasure and instruction"; Hawthorne's work had run into his "blood and bones" and even out of his "fingers' ends." But Tuckerman made the presentation diffidently, explaining that he claimed little for his poems; he described them as "New Englandy" and hoped that they might deserve Hawthorne's favorable opinion. He confided that he planned "to have the book published in England (if it seem worthy), as here I fancy it would be but coldly received."[1]

Within two weeks Hawthorne replied that he thought the volume remarkable, but he, too, questioned "whether the poems will obtain a very early or wide recognition from the public, either in England or America." He based his judgment on the belief that their merit "does not lie upon the surface, but must be looked for with faith and sympathy, and a kind of insight as when you look into a carbuncle to discover its hidden fire." With frankness and sympathy he said that he foresaw clearly a major stumbling block: "The great difficulty with you will be, to get yourself read at all; if you could be read twice, the book might be a success; but who reads (in a way that deserves to be called reading) so much as once, in these days?" He was impressed a good deal by "The Stranger," "Picomegan," "Margites," and by the whole series of sonnets.

Unlike Hawthorne, who had read and reread most of the poems, Emerson centered his attention on the conventional pieces only. The volume gave him "great pleasure—more than [he] dared hope for in opening it." As stated earlier, he liked "Rhotruda," and after that, "Mark Atherton," "The Stranger," "The School-Girl," and "Elidore." He noted Tuckerman's "love of native flowers," his "skill to name them," and his "delight in words that are melodies." Even though Emerson warned him of the difficulty of achieving poetic success, he encouraged him to seek a wider audience by a general publication and to permit Fields to print "Rhotruda" in the *Atlantic* to announce "the arrival of what is so rich and rare."

There was more that Emerson wanted to say about the book, but refrained; he told Tuckerman that "when we ride again in a train together I hope you will give me a chance to say it"; but he considered the book important enough to note it in his *Journal*. Here he recorded a conversation with Ellery Channing who was ill disposed toward the new poet. Except for two or three good lines and meters and a "refined and delicate" general impression, Channing found nothing worth reading. His chief complaint was the strong Tennysonian flavor. "Young poets," he complained, "run on a notion that they must name the flowers, talk about an orchis, and say something about Indians." Emerson quoted Channing as saying, "I prefer passion and sense and genius to botany." Channing's well-known anti-Tennysonian bias accounts for this comment: "Ellery says of Tennyson, 'What is best, is the things he don't [*sic*] say.'"[2]

Emerson's failure to mention the sonnets to Tuckerman drew a request that he read them; but, when Emerson was ready to comply, he found that his copy was missing. He thought Fields might know of its whereabouts, but Fields thought that James Russell Lowell had it. Emerson said to Lowell, "The poet, in sending me his book requested my attention to the 'Sonnets,' which I have not yet read." This note is dated June 18, 1861, and Emerson had written his first letter to Tuckerman on March 28, 1861; it is clear, therefore, he had felt no urgency to read the sonnets. There is no direct evidence that they ever discussed the volume or the sonnets again, but there is no doubt that Tuckerman later learned about the lost volume because, in April of 1863, just after the London edition appeared, he sent Emerson a copy to replace the missing one. In the accompanying letter he wrote, "I have not forgotten your kind words of encouragement and approval, or the stamp of valuation that you affixed." Whether this remark refers to the original commentary or to a later one is not clear. At any rate, Emerson kept the new volume and it is still in his library in the museum of the Concord Antiquarian Society in Concord.

James T. Fields liked much of Tuckerman's work and supported his judgment by printing "Rhotruda" and asking about the possibility of using "Margites" and the untitled, "I took from its glass a flower."[3] And, in a general and guarded statement, Longfellow observed that the poems "are thoughtful and full of feeling; and breathe an air of the country, an odor of farms, which is healthy and suggestive of strength."

When Jones Very was asked if he would accept a copy of the poems, he replied graciously that he would and that he was pleased to hear from his former student whose "appearance when a freshman" he could still recall.[4] After reading the volume, he sent a most encouraging letter. The "description of our natural scenery, and of our wild plants and flowers" brought to his mind days spent wandering in pastures with his brother who "no longer walks with me here on the earth." But Very's sensitive and appreciative comments were reserved for the sonnets:

> Your sonnets tell of grief but purified and consoled by faith, which alone can sustain us in life's trial and give us peace. As, in your 28th sonnet, 1st part, you hint the great objects of faith, God, Christ, a Spiritual and eternal state give rest to the mind, and heart and these alone. The concluding sonnets of the 2nd part, 34th, 35th, and 36th are beautifully expressed and call forth my deepest sympathy with your loss, and with the faith which sustains you.

As a token of appreciation, he sent a copy of his sister's poems to his former student and invited him to come to Salem.

The religious faith and the spiritual strength which Very felt in the sonnets and of which he so warmly approved were differently regarded by another former teacher, Bishop Hopkins of Vermont, who sympathized with the poet on the death of his wife but charged him with idolatry and urged him to see the folly of human love that usurped the place of the divine. Eschewing other commentary, the Bishop took this opportunity to write a windy sermon. The accusation of idolatry so disturbed Tuckerman that he told Hawthorne about the "cleric critic" who had misread the sonnets, had accused him of idolatry, and had caustically remarked "that *Margites* would have been much better employed in some work of Christian usefullness."

Henry T. Tuckerman, the popular writer and critic, was Tuckerman's cousin; and the poet took advantage of this relationship to solicit not only his opinion but also that of Bryant, with whom H. T. Tuckerman was closely associated. The result was a tangled correspondence in which the critic offered his view and then quoted from a note he had received from Bryant. H. T. Tuckerman's comments were based on his understanding of the "average standard of sympathy among lovers of poetry." He charged his cousin with being "too exclusive a disciple of a class of poets" which consisted of Wordsworth, Keats, and Tennyson; he suggested that the directness and "clear emphatic style of Pope, Gray and Campbell" would essentially promote "a quicker appreciation and recognition of the poet's merits." He believed that, as exposition of personal feelings, the poems were often graceful and genuine but that their scope and details of natural beauty were too narrow and that success depended on a much wider range. From the technical point of view, he said that he "perceived many peculiarities of expression" which struck him as defects.

The Tennysonian influence to which this critic had objected was echoed by Bryant who recognized that Tuckerman's charm and his claim to originality were derived from "a strong love of Nature and a remarkable perception of her beauties," but who also felt that these excellent qualities were overshadowed by "thought that is too dreamy and mystical" and by the poet's allowing the reader to too often "perceive that he has been a diligent student and an intense admirer of Tennyson."

H. T. Tuckerman was instrumental in eliciting a comment from George Ripley, whose remarks were forwarded to Greenfield. Ripley's observations were a mixture of praise and fault-finding. His impression was that the poet was "imbued with the spirit" of Wordsworth and exhibited "fidelity and skill" in seizing upon "those aspects of Nature that appeal to the imagination." His use of New England scenery matched Bryant's, and he had transformed it "into golden materials for his thoughtful and suggestive verse." Ripley recognized the genuine feeling of pathos and tenderness; he approved of the expressions of sentiment because they were not "inflated, forced or artificial." On the other hand, even though the poems showed harmony of versification and theme, they were "certainly too harsh and rugged for the popular taste—perhaps, indeed, for any taste." The chief faults, he found, were "unnecessary inversions, in the use of unheard of and unattractive words and phrases and too heavy an accumulation of epithets and illustrations." Ripley's conclusion was that Tuckerman had a "true poetic view, and a richness of thought and sentiment" marred by execution which "needs toning down and pruning of eccentric turns and phrases." The H. T. Tuckerman-Bryant-Ripley commentaries, though less polite than those of Hawthorne, Emerson, and Longfellow, contained sufficient praise to make their adverse remarks palatable.

Another correspondent was George S. Hillard, an old Boston friend, who wrote a long, detailed letter. He, too, saw the power and genius; he marked the fine perceptions of natural beauty, tenderness, and delicacy of feeling; he applauded the rare "skill in wielding the resources of our language." But he complained that the volume was overburdened by the "influence of a recluse life" and was made uneven by "the want of a strict mental training early in life." In addition, he said that the observations were too minute, had too much of individual detail, and carried "the descriptive element too far." More seriously, he found fault with the style because it sometimes lacked clarity and needed lightening and bracing. Hillard, like other critics, stressed the point that a demand for careful, serious reading which a busy age was unprepared to give was the great obstacle to popular success. Moderns will not read "what takes them any trouble to comprehend." For illustration, he cited Bryant and Longfellow and said that their popularity was based on an easy comprehension owing to clarity of style and lack of great originality. He granted that Tuckerman had originality and poetic genius, but he urged him to balance these with more patience and attention to style and expression.[5]

Although letters from American writers have been preserved, not a single one from British poets survives. Tennyson, who was at the head of the list of those to whom he had sent copies, surely must have replied. Yet search for such material has been fruitless. Sophia Eckley had told the Brownings of her brother's volume, and she reported to him that they were "full of interest to see" it. If the Brownings had anything to say, there is no record of it; even Sophia is silent on this point. What the Rossetti family and W. S. Landor of the Florentine coterie thought of the poems is unknown too, even though Sophia said that "all my friends know of its appearance." An exception was Annabella Noel, Byron's granddaughter, a "sympathizing reader"; her nice note to the poet was enclosed with a letter Sophia had sent to her brother.

The effusive letters from his sister in Florence tell of her delight in reading the poems and of her greater delight in making his work known to members of her circle; but her comments are nothing more than a series of joyous utterances. She had been familiar with his writings well before the 1860 edition, but she was hardly prepared for poems of such dazzling beauty. "I did not know that you had so much *power, Genius,*" she wrote. She fancied she would be reading dreamy lyrics; instead, she found works with stern and grand thoughts. His "fearlessness in the use of words" was extraordinary and his "graphic, witty and exquisite lines" impressed her very much. Such little commentary from abroad is unfortunate, but sufficient material from writers at home compensates partially for it.

The flurry of correspondence indicated that Tuckerman had little chance to achieve quick popularity or even slow recognition in his own day. Only a few of the conventional poems were used in the literary magazines; the rest were generally unnoticed. The even-tempered expression and Augustan clarity as found in "Rhotruda," "The Clearing," and "Picomegan" suited public taste; the sonnets were too elusive or strange to win serious contemporary attention. The poet had marched a step ahead of his age and had to wait for time to catch up with him.

III   *The 1863 and the 1864 Editions*

"Keen, brilliant, shallow, with a ready phrase"

When reviewers in England presented their judgments of the London edition, their comments paralleled those of the American critics.[6] They praised Tuckerman's acute eye in describing what was to them a remote and distant place where nature abounded with strange, exotic plants and flowers. The reviewer in *The Parthenon* welcomed the poet's serene voice as great relief from the "inharmonious verse" and martial music raised by the tumult of war, and he requested a charitable hearing for a poet who "warbles his native wood-notes in an unfamiliar land." The novelty of details and the "vague pictures of the skies and landscapes of the western world" appealed to him. Here was a naturalist-poet whose work showed evidence of "good taste and genuine feeling," but the sonnets were merely "often graceful and pathetic" and without "any great amount of poetic merit."

In *John Bull,* the reviewer noted with approval Tuckerman's familiarity with "Nature in the back-woods" and "with his imagery and illustrations drawn from the American continent." He stated that the book contained some very spirited verse and some excellent lines in the Hudibrastic tradition, but the poetry was at times marred by such rhymes as "border" and "broader." The sonnets were passed over without comment.

The *Spectator's* reviewer thought that the rhymes would not satisfy a sternly critical ear but commended the poet on his ability to create picturesque word-painting. Facetiously, he wondered if this unknown poet might "possibly be an American writer." The whimsical review in *The Guardian* reported "some power of imitation and flow of language, some grave thoughts and solemn memories, and occasional bursts of high spirits" and concluded archly that in "the seats of high civilization Mr. Tuckerman may be accepted as a thoughtful man, but he must also be considered as rather a rustical poet."

The critic for *Athenaeum* was pleased with the clarity of some of the conventional pieces but was annoyed by obscurity and diffusion scattered throughout the book. The reviewer in *The London Reader* attacked the poems on the grounds of their discursiveness and deplored the lack of "coherence, distinctness and appropriateness." He saw Tuckerman's almost boundless command of words, a command which did not prevent him from "frequently employing most barbarous and inappropriate terms and phrases." Uncouth phraseology, he added, was scattered throughout the volume. He commended the more easily grasped poems but avoided making specific comments on the more difficult sonnets. Most serious attacks on Tuckerman's obscurity appeared in *The London Review,* whose critic granted that not all the poems were "hopelessly abstruse" and not without "the true poetic ring," but that he was too often baffled "in spite of the most earnest endeavours to discover what the author means." For opacity of meaning he singled out the ill-fated "The starry flower, the flower-like stars that fade"; it was a "perplexing puzzle."

No British critic thought the volume worth elaborate consideration or detailed study; instead, there were only these quite brief notices. From them it is clear that no one was prepared to give Tuckerman more than passing recognition; at best, the critics thought him a talented versifier and a harbinger of strange sights from remote New England. Nevertheless, such tepid reception did not deter Fields from bringing out the first American edition in 1864.

In the *Atlantic*, it received a cordial acceptance. The poet was commended for his "minute knowledge of the peculiarities of the natural world as it appears in New England."[7] At the same time, he was reproved for "drawing too largely upon this source of interest." The sonnets were praised for their "thought and expression," "tenderness and sensibility," but the praise was tempered with the warning that "strings which vibrate such music should be sparingly struck." The review in the Boston *Evening Transcript* was like the one in the *Atlantic*.[8] It agreed that Tuckerman's "knowledge of New England nature is singularly exact, and many a flower and weed . . . makes . . . its first appearance in verse"; it said that traces of "deep thought and deep sensibility," especially in the sonnets, were not the results of mere play of mind but records of what the poet had actually experienced. Sincerity, depth, "imaginative felicities of epithet and image" gave freshness to the volume. For evidence of Tuckerman's poetic feeling and power, attention was invited to "November," "April," "Inspiration," "Infatuation," "Rhotruda," and "Coralie." The general impression was that—despite disfiguration of verse, clumsy turns of thought, and personal caprice —the book was that of "a recluse whose observation has been directed on nature and his own heart rather than on the busy world, and who has learned by this communion many a secret which is hidden from less secluded spirits."

The Springfield *Daily Republican* carried a brief comment that the "smooth and musical structure" was marred by a "certain vagueness and dreaminess that leaves the reader in doubt as to the writer's meaning." The reviewer had apparently

abandoned hope of understanding Tuckerman because he blithe-
ly dismissed the volume by calling it "a collection of light musical idylls as seasonable midsummer reading."

Much more discerning and appreciative was the reviewer in
the New York *Tribune* who said that the poems "abound in
finely conceived images and passages of rare beauty" but upon
occasion lacked artistic treatment and were deficient in "fully
sustained idea." Although disturbed by the lack of completeness,
he recognized that Tuckerman was much more than a mere
versifier, writing jingles in dull phrases about flowers. As an
example he quoted this passage from "The School-Girl":

> . . . So her young life,
> Above the gulf, detached, and yet detained,
> Suspended swung; as o'er a fresh-fallen pool
> A laurel-blossom, loosened by the rain,
> Hangs at its pistil-thread,—hangs, shakes, and falls.[9]

It was, in his opinion, a rare poet who could turn the laurel
disengaging its corolla into poetry. He perceived a vigorous
freshness infused into a place where

> . . . breathes the scented pyrola, and there
> The perfect fragrance of the partridge-flower,
> 'Mid moss, and maiden-hair, and damp dead leaves.[10]

With a good show of tolerance and kindly resignation he mentioned the influence of Tennyson, calling it a disease which
had to run its course: "This seems to be the inexorable fate of
all our young poets. This is so inevitable that for our own part,
we have left off complaining of it; and, when there is promise
of future excellence in one of the class, only wait resignedly his
convalescence."

IV *The Rediscovery*

"The hidden Spring"

It was inevitable that Tuckerman's poems should quickly disappear from sight and remain hidden for almost half a century.
Everything militated against their recovery. His early disengage-
ment from active participation in the busy life that swirled past
him, his very slender literary output that had had a lukewarm
reception, and his unorthodox treatment of the sonnet almost

encouraged total obscurity. Added to these obstacles was the
fact that some of his best work never appeared in print while
he was alive. These are sufficient reasons to account for his
fading absolutely from notice in the last quarter of the nineteenth century.

The recovery of his poems led to the discovery of the posthumous works; by means of both events together, Tuckerman
was rescued from oblivion, and good luck played its capricious
role in each case. Louis How's unpublished collection of little-
known American poetry contained two of Tuckerman's sonnets;
Walter Prichard Eaton read them and was impressed. But by
1908 Tuckerman's *Poems* was so hard to find that it took a
Boston book dealer a year to locate a copy. By then Eaton had
almost forgotten the matter. Had the book dealer been less in-
dustrious and less persistent, the volume might never have
reached Eaton, and there is a good chance that Tuckerman
would still be unknown. On such a slender thread hung his
rediscovery.[11]

Without Eaton's lively essay in *Forum* (January, 1909), the
Tuckerman family might have done nothing at that time to
resuscitate his work. Also, their efforts might have been less
concerted without the encouragement provided by the fact that
the manuscripts and papers had been preserved despite mis-
management in connection with the settlement of the estate.[12]
Most likely all the materials had been moved from Greenfield
to Amherst by his brother, Edward. The poet's son, Frederick,
was only sixteen years old when his father died; therefore, it is
unlikely that he had a hand in taking care of anything. But in
1873 he was living in his uncle's house in Amherst and surely
knew of the existence of his father's papers. When his uncle died
in 1886, he gained possession of this material and wisely kept
it. Thus, when his wife, his daughter, and Witter Bynner wanted
to examine the long-forgotten papers, they were readily avail-
able. They could easily have disappeared or have been destroyed
—and much of the best work would have been lost. But again
good fortune prevailed.

On these two fortuitous circumstances depends the inclusion
of Tuckerman's name in American literature. Credit for the
revival and renewal of interest must be given to both Eaton and
Bynner. The greater share belongs to Bynner, but without
Eaton's curiosity and enthusiasm probably nothing would have

taken place in 1909 to initiate the resultant activity. Eaton's aim in writing his article was exceedingly modest. All he wanted to do was to "shed a tiny ray back" upon the memory of Tuckerman, who was, he thought, too good a poet to be completely forgotten. In the beginning, he did not treat his subject with zeal or overexaggeration; he was a bit skeptical about the "nuggets of pure gold" which the volume was supposed to contain. However, his skepticism gave way to genuine enthusiasm when he found not only the promised nuggets but also a potential lode.

Eaton disapproved of Tuckerman's lack of sustained style, of his crudities, of his "imperfect poetic faculty." He believed the unorthodox handling of the sonnet resulted from a scorn for or ignorance of the poetic form, and he termed the running together of two sonnets an "unfortunate trick." Yet, despite these serious faults and qualifications, he could find one sonnet "touched with fire from the high altar" which glittered with "hints of an imagination that missed by ever so little poetic greatness"; another which showed "flashes of pure gold in his [Tuckerman's] imagination"; a third which possessed such passion and sincerity that "it stabs." Ranging through the lyrics, Eaton approved of the careful handling of plants and flowers, of the "powers of observation of natural effects," and of the ability to turn a melancholy mood into something "piercing and beautiful." For support, he reprinted excerpts from "May flowers," "The Question," "The School-Girl," and "Margites."

In addition to these samplings, he selected six complete sonnets as specimens of the "pure gold." Unaware of the parodic treatment once accorded the sonnet, "The starry flower, the flower-like stars that fade," he performed a valuable service by showing that this sonnet is linked with the one that follows; and, as a result of his reprinting both, he could point with good reason to the imaginative flash in the opening lines of the second sonnet:

> And so, as this great sphere (now turning slow
> Up to the light from that abyss of stars,
> Now wheeling into gloom through sunset bars)[13]

He closed his essay by wondering why "I took from its glass a flower" had been so utterly ignored when so many inferior poems were still preserved in anthologies.

Part of Eaton's great contribution in behalf of Tuckerman was his restraint in meting out praise. By pointing to what he considered serious shortcomings and by permitting the gold of the best work to shine through, he let Tuckerman speak for himself— a most judicious move. By lavish use of examples, he exposed some poems to the light they had so long been denied. How far he exceeded his modest aim and how successfully his "tiny ray" illuminated the forgotten poetry can best be measured by the importance of Witter Bynner's *The Sonnets of Frederick Goddard Tuckerman* (1931).

In the same year that Eaton's essay appeared, the cache of Tuckerman's work was discovered. It contained notebooks, commonplace books, scraps of verse, several incomplete narrative poems, *The Cricket*, and the forty-one sonnets which made up Parts III, IV, and V of the sequences.[14] When Bynner first read the newly unearthed sonnets, he thought that they were roughly hewn and inferior to those published in 1860; but, upon reconsideration, he concluded that "the poet's mastery had not lessened" and that the rough texture was exactly what Tuckerman had deliberately designed. By adding these to the two published series, Bynner was convinced that the five sequences deserved an honored niche in American literature. After a lapse of twenty-one years, he brought out the edition of the sonnets destined to be the foundation upon which Tuckerman's reputation was to be built.

The excellent preface had a biographical sketch, an appraisal of all the poems, a refutation of many of Eaton's charges, and an evaluation of the sonnets. Bynner agreed with Eaton that many lyrics and narratives were mediocre and should be ignored; but, at the same time, he regarded several worth preserving in whole or in part. Into his essay he incorporated the first sixteen lines from "The School-Girl," all of "I took from its glass a flower," "The Question," "Refrigerium," and "Margites." In his opinion these were well worth keeping alive. Like Eaton, he saw dazzling lines that flashed throughout the otherwise colorless poems, and he printed several examples.

Bynner objected strongly to Eaton's critical strictures that the sonnets were metrically faulty, that they were deficient in form and style, and that they reflected the poet's misuse of the sonnet form itself. His refutation was based on the belief that Tuckerman was an experimenter in verse much like Walt

Whitman and Emily Dickinson; that he knew exactly what he was doing when he ended a sonnet with an Alexandrine or with a shortened line. He argued that Tuckerman deviated from traditional rhyme-schemes "to suit the roll and rise and fall of his meaning" and that by his bold innovations he was not mutilating the form but was reinvigorating it. For more evidence of Tuckerman's deliberate experimenting, Bynner pointed to the invention of words to match exactly the mood, to the "re-syllabling of words," and to the use of an apparently private mythology.

Bynner was so impressed that he was pleased to announce that this sonneteer was "not only the peer of his great contemporaries but the equal of his most important successors." To support such high claim, he invited special attention to Sonnets XXVI and XXVII in Part I; to Sonnets VI and X in Part II; to Sonnets II, III, VIII, and X in Part III; and to Sonnets II, III, and XVI in Part V. His final assessment was that "Tuckerman's sonnets rank with the noblest in the language and dignify America with poems not bettered in their kind by anyone of his time or since."

Such high praise for an unknown poet was bound to attract the attention of reviewers. It was important news when a poet-critic of Bynner's stature would unequivocally announce the appearance on the literary scene of a neglected poet who was rightfully entitled to the first rank among American writers. Among the reviewer-critics who took notice were Theodore Morrison, William Rose Benét, Eda Lou Walton, and Ben Ray Redman; in addition, there were unsigned reviews in *The New Republic,* the New York *Times,* and the Boston *Evening Transcript.* All the reviews, brief but cogent, expressed general agreement that Tuckerman merited recognition; but reviewers were hesitant to agree fully with Bynner's accolade.

The sole reviewer in complete agreement was Eda Lou Walton. In *The Nation* of September 2, 1931, she said that, to her, Tuckerman was as great a poet as Bynner had stated; and she even suggested that he had not gone far enough. She compared the fate that had overtaken Tuckerman with that which had enveloped Whitman and Dickinson. She accounted for their neglect by pointing out that all three were outside the limit of literary tradition of the mid-century and, specifically, that Tuckerman's poetic voice was entirely his own and did not depend upon English letters and poetry for subject matter or craftsmanship.

She was acutely aware of his personal grief, which he had expressed with sensitivity, and of his brooding thoughts; she recognized the existence of a poet whose eyes regarded the natural scene as it really existed. He was, in this instance, superior to many of his contemporaries, who looked at nature "in romantic guise." His ability to transfer emotion through homely experience reminded her of Emily Dickinson's imagery. She approved of his swift images and clear exposition of deep thought. She said he was a poet of such great attainment that "we should do well to list him with his contemporaries, and perhaps above them, although he wrote so little." Her enthusiastic review included Sonnet XIV, Part II, and Sonnet III, Part V, as illustrations of this form not surpassed in the poet's time or in the first three decades of the twentieth century.

Theodore Morrison, writing in *The Bookman* (April, 1931), readily acknowledged that Tuckerman was a true poet. He agreed with Bynner that unusual handling of the sonnet form revealed neither ignorance nor indifference, as Eaton had suggested, but strength which molded the form to suit personal needs and still maintain its basic character. He judged that the greatest worth of the sonnets derived from consideration of them singly or in small groups. He thought that the total impression fell short of full success, partly because "their intellectual promise" remained unfulfilled and partly because Tuckerman lacked a universal voice and his emotion was more a matter of morbidity than of grief. Although Morrison could not agree entirely with Bynner, he could concur with an evaluation which described Tuckerman as "an original and gifted poet, with great strength and beauty of imagination." The final judgment in this review was that "those who write of American poetry in the future will accord him a place of genuine honor."

In *The Saturday Review of Literature* (February 7, 1931), William Rose Benét wrote in praise of the sonnets but was wary of Bynner's critical judgment. He noted irregularities and conceded that they were deliberate and studied but felt that they were not always successful. He said that the strength in the sonnets was to be found in "striking lines and phrases," in sharp observation of natural surroundings, and in the "feeling for words in their sound, in their connotations, in their very shape and form." These qualities entitled Tuckerman to be called a true poet. As an example of striking imagination, Benét reprinted Sonnet VIII, Part III, and, as an illustration of close observation of nature, Sonnet X, Part IV. Benét intimated that he could not place Tuckerman quite so high in the poetic scale as had Bynner, but he was pleased to know of a new poet deserving of recognition.

The reviewer in *The New Republic* (November 18, 1931), in a general remark, described the work as "one of the most interesting sonnet sequences in English literature." He noted how their subjective orientation and sad tone were offset by their dignity and found the sonnets "extraordinarily sensitive to the spectacles and events of Nature," embellished with "verbal music" of a high order. And, in the New York *Times Book Review* (May 24, 1931), the reviewer expressed the opinion that the neglect of Tuckerman was tragic and that many of the poems were much too good to have been overlooked by anthologists. Tuckerman's power was best measured by its ability to capture the "fleeting moment." He contended that Bynner's assessment was acceptable if limited to American sonneteers of that time—a period in American literature not notable for its sonnets. The sonnets missed complete possession of the structural beauty which gives character to the form; the irregularities so twisted the structure that his sonnets might be thought of as lyrics of fourteen lines in iambic pentameter and, in this light, became "something memorable . . . something almost precious."

In the Boston *Evening Transcript* (June 6, 1931), the reviewer saw a sentimental strain in the sonnets and observed that they "will bring tears to the eyes and a catch in the voice of him who reads understandingly and sympathetically." The poet's "brooding bafflement about the meaning of life remains an unanswered question even in this more modern age." In his opinion, the poems were destined to have a long life because they had already outlived the age in which they were written.

Ben Ray Redman, writing in the New York *Herald Tribune Books* of June 7, 1931, said that Tuckerman was too fine a poet to be lost, but that was as far as he cared to go. He directed his remarks to Bynner's essay as much as to the sonnets and found both deficient. He charged Bynner with claiming too much for the poet; he refused to believe that Tuckerman ought to be compared to Milton or Wordsworth even though Bynner had suggested such a comparison when he wrote that the sonnets "rank with the noblest in the language." In Redman's judgment, they were not worthy of even the second place; the best of Drayton, Daniel, and Drummond outranked Tuckerman. He chided Bynner by reminding him that "injudicious praise serves an author ill." When Redman turned to the sonnets themselves, he granted Tuckerman the right to poetic freedom but wanted to know exactly what had been accomplished. He complained about the rhymes and selected Sonnet XV, Part III, as an example of monotony "produced by successions of similar vowel sounds." His conclusion was that "Tuckerman's mind and personality were sufficiently interesting to make his struggle worthy of remembrance, but the struggle did not end in full mastery for the poet."

In addition to these public reviews and impressions, there were two private observations in letters to Witter Bynner, who had sent out presentation copies to friends and had asked for comments. In the copy to Edwin Arlington Robinson he wrote on the flyleaf, "What do you think of him?" Examination of Robinson's copy, now lodged in the Library at Colby College, Maine, reveals that the book shows very little evidence of wear and that Robinson never went beyond page 127, the end of Part III. Most of the remaining pages are uncut, and those that Robinson may have read are innocent of underscorings or marginal notations.[15] However, in response to Bynner's query, he wrote that he "enjoyed and admired" the sonnets but could not "rate them quite as high as you [Bynner] do" even though they did have "astonishing good lines." While by no means denying Robinson's greatness, Bynner is convinced that Tuckerman and Robinson are at "the very top of American poets, with Tuckerman perhaps a bit ahead of Robinson for sheer genius— or possibly it's neck and neck." A second response came from Robert Frost, who made this precise observation: "They have high lines that a blind man could feel with his fingers."[16]

The consensus was that Bynner had somewhat overstated the case, but had performed a valuable service in reviving a poet who deserved to be included among the better New England poets of the nineteenth century. The most tangible result of the 1931 edition and the attendant reviews was the initial appearance of Tuckerman's sonnets in anthologies. Perhaps the first anthologists to do honor to him were Benét and Norman Holmes Pearson, who chose the two sonnets Benét had printed in his 1931 review along with four more to include in the *Oxford Anthology of American Literature* (1938). To justify having included him, they noted that Tuckerman was a poet whose sonnets were in advance of his own time to such an extent that they might be "close to what the nineteenth century would have considered anti-poetic."

In his *An Anthology of the New England Poets from Colonial Times to the Present Day* (1948), Louis Untermeyer included six sonnets. Tuckerman was placed in the section entitled "Full Flower" with Bryant, Emerson, Longfellow, Whittier, Thoreau, and others. However, Untermeyer chose to list him as one of the "rarely encountered but remarkable poets" like Edward Taylor and Jones Very. He thought that Tuckerman was worthy of notice because his "sonnets have genuine distinction." His judgment of them was fairly close to Bynner's when he said that "Tuckerman shifted the traditional rhyme-scheme to fit his shifting moods." He especially appreciated the apparent roughness of texture because this quality gave "homely strength" to work which was a pleasant contrast to the "overfastidiousness and overpolished grace" usually encountered in the second half of the nineteenth century.[17] The sonnets he chose were: Sonnets I, V, X, XII, and XIX, Part I; and Sonnet XVII, Part II.

George F. Whicher included all twenty-eight sonnets of Part I in his anthology, *Poetry of the New England Renaissance* (1950). Like other commentators, he noted the "highly unorthodox handling of rhyme schemes" and the "brilliantly original imagery" used to "analyze and objectify his grief." Tuckerman's search for ways of expression reminded him of Eliot's "objective correlative." While much of the poetry was unsure and weak, the "sonnets reached moments of sheer loveliness such as one associates with sophisticated and slightly decadent poets like Edward Fitzgerald or Ernest Dowson." Whicher called him "a strange exotic in the Connecticut Valley."[18]

A major contributor to the renaissance of Tuckerman was Yvor Winters; as far back as 1938, Winters was moved to state in *Maule's Curse* that "Tuckerman is unquestionably a distinguished poet" and that he is "much like the Hawthorne of the last romances, except that he writes better."¹⁹ When *The Cricket* was published in 1950, Professor Winters took the occasion to discuss the sonnets and *The Cricket* in some detail. In the *Hudson Review* (Autumn, 1950), he saw in the emergence of Tuckerman one more piece of evidence to support his thesis that the history of American literature will "have to be drastically revised." He thought the poetry was "decadent, sophisticated with respect to the qualities which it actually possesses, sensuously rich, and too often somewhat careless." But the sonnets are "so lovely as to deserve a high place in our poetic literature of the nineteenth century." He directed special attention to Sonnets XVI and XVII, Part II, because they were the most beautiful; and he included excerpts from them in his essay. Acutely aware of fine lines of "great beauty," he also found passages spoiled by "facile phrasing." After summarizing and briefly commenting on the five sections of *The Cricket,* Winters was impelled to declare that "it is one of the great meditations on death to be written since the seventeenth century, along with *Le Cimetière Marin, Sunday Morning* and *Thanatopsis.*" In his opinion *The Cricket* "is probably the greatest single American poem of the nineteenth century; and the British poems of the same period which can be compared with it are few indeed."²⁰ However, in his critical foreword to Momaday's book, fifteen years later, his assessment of this poem is that it is "the greatest poem in English of the century."

A major step toward a greater appreciation of Tuckerman's work is Mordecai Marcus's essay, "The Poetry of Frederick Goddard Tuckerman: A Reconsideration" printed in *Discourse* (Concordia College, Moorhead, Minnesota) in the winter issue of 1961-62. This detailed, perceptive, and sympathetic article deals with an analysis of several of the sonnets and of *The Cricket.* He saw four major themes: the "sense of personal inadequacies"; the mourning over the loss of his wife; the search for value in his own existence; and the scanning of the American scene and the evoking of "local history and cultural change." Marcus focused his attention on Sonnets VII and XIII, Part I; Sonnets I, XIV, XVI, and XIX, Part II; and on Sonnets IV, VII, and XVI, Part V. This selection was generous enough to include a variety of views of the ideas in the sonnets and of Tuckerman's technical handling of his material. He noted the variations in language to suit the mood; pointed to the colloquial phrases in Sonnet I, Part II; to the subtleties in Sonnet XIV, Part II; and to the occasional harsh word to help a shifting mood, as in Sonnet IV, Part V. He found the imagery rich and the use of metaphor exact and effective; he found, at times, that when metaphor gives way to symbol, Tuckerman "achieves his most brilliant effects." All the sonnets, however, are not of equally high value in form, in thought, or in expression of feeling. There are weaknesses in some of the better sonnets and, in lesser ones, "discursiveness, trite phrasing, uncontrolled self-pity, and lack of dramatic or symbolic unity."

Professor Marcus lavished high praise on *The Cricket*—not, perhaps, so high as Yvor Winters had. Considered to be Tuckerman's greatest accomplishment, the poem is analyzed systematically to show how the cricket is used symbolically as the messenger of death and as "the ambiguous radiance of life." He cites examples of "subtle dramatic contrast" and "functional metrical variation." The fourth section is compared to a minuet as it gracefully "imparts tenderness and resignation in the face of strife and loss." The fifth part, although lacking in clarity and organization, is the "most beautifully written part of the poem." He notes some obscurity, archaic diction, and insufficient transition between sections—characteristics which might detract from quick acceptance by twentieth-century readers. Nevertheless, the strengths outweigh the weaknesses. Its beauty lies in the use of language, the skill in development of the theme, the musical variations, and the masterful handling of the material. Marcus closed his essay with the note that a full consideration of Tuckerman's poetry will have to be postponed until the sonnets and *The Cricket* have attained wider recognition through more generous anthologizing. In the history of the revival of interest in Tuckerman's work, this essay is of prime import and is, itself, worthy of wider circulation than it has had heretofore.[21]

A recent and most influential notice is in Edmund Wilson's *Patriotic Gore* (1962). He touched the heart of the problem which has retarded Tuckerman's public acceptance when he said: "It is easier to give an idea of Frederick Tuckerman's little grotesqueries than to illustrate his peculiar excellence. One has really to read his poems in sequence." Wilson was drawn to the sonnets because of their surprisingly sharp phrasing, their "individual flavor," and their success in using homely images effectively; these characteristics endow them with "freshness and felicity." He said that, out of the natural material Tuckerman had found in Hancock County and on Long Island, he had built a "magic kingdom" which was "alive to beauty." This private world was more genuine than was Emily Dickinson's, which, Wilson believes, would have quickly vanished had she been encouraged to publish. But Tuckerman built his own world, populated it with obscure characters from the Bible and antiquity, and spoke there in such quiet tones that some of the "occasional obscurity . . . contributes to one's general impression of a soliloquy not quite overheard."

The idea that Tuckerman invented his own mythology is considered in Wilson's commentary. He associates this observation with the frequency in American literature of the creation of mythological worlds in Washington Irving's Rip Van Winkle and Sleepy Hollow, in Longfellow's borrowings from Schoolcraft in Michigan, in Poe's "dark tarn of Auber and the ghoul-haunted woodland of Weir," and in Cabell's Poictesme. Wilson mildly complains about Tuckerman's allusions because some are so obscure as to sound like inventions and others, he thought, were figments; and Eponina, Actia, Arlotte, Mandané, Dagoraus Whear are cited as examples. But Tuckerman wrote "remarkable poetry" which departed from the traditional ways of his older, more famous contemporaries. The sonnets make up a "strange journal . . . of recollections still heart-breakingly vivid, of 'weeping solitudes,' country sights, country weather"; they have a "touch of the fantastic" but are realistic. Wilson notes Tuckerman's irregular handling of the sonnet form, the departure from the usual rhyme-schemes, the truncated lines, and the break from exact form by not adhering to the ordinary separation of the sestet and the octet. But these deviations did not particularly annoy him; his critical judgment placed a most favorable stamp on the poetry. In the course of his remarks, Wilson used for illustration all of Sonnet XXXVII, Part II; Sonnet I, Part II; and the final three sonnets of Part V.[22]

The Complete Poems of Frederick Goddard Tuckerman, edited by N. Scott Momaday, appeared in 1965. This edition continues the evidence of mounting interest in the poet; and, for the first time, all the poems are readily accessible. This volume, a valuable contribution, substantiates the need to provide Tuckerman with a wider audience. Momaday's introduction contains some biographical material, some observations on Tuckerman's relationship to the intellectual milieu of his day, and an appreciation of his view on nature. In discussing Tuckerman and Emerson, Momaday believes that they "were at odds on the most fundamental points." Basing his arguments principally on Emerson's *Nature,* Momaday notes three essential differences: Where "Emerson recommends solitude explicitly," Tuckerman "may be said to recommend solitude implicitly and by example"; where Emerson attaches great importance to the landscape as "a barometer of moral change," Tuckerman holds the position that nature does not and cannot reflect such change; and, where Emerson insists on the need and the value of intuition and of mysticism, Tuckerman demonstrates that in nature there are, in the main, only unfathomable contradictions. On the basis of these differences, Momaday concludes that Tuckerman's affinity with the tenets of Emersonian Romanticism is superficial. He writes that Tuckerman "stands in historical opposition to the mainstream of nineteenth-century American Romanticism."

Long a champion of Tuckerman, Yvor Winters wrote a critical foreword to Momaday's book, in which he asserts that Tuckerman's true relationship is bound up with post-Romantic English and French poetry. Most of Winters's comments are a rewording of what he had said in 1950 in his essay on *The Cricket.* In the New York *Times Book Review* (June 20, 1965), Richard Eberhart says that Tuckerman did not point to the future but looked back to the eighteenth century. In general, he approves of the poems, but he apparently does not consider them anything more than gentle evocations of the past: "His is a low-keyed poetry written with extreme patience, deep understanding of self, a gentle awareness unpressured by the outside world. It lives in a rich ambience of the past." As for matters of style, Eberhart sees the poet as a quietist, writing with "little technical invention" and in "old fashioned . . . style and tone."

Irving Howe, in the *New York Review of Books* (March 25, 1965), is much more explicit. His reading of the poems leads him to note that the sonnets, despite excessive stylistic flaws, are Tuckerman's most distinguished works; in them, by eschewing the mystic, the exalted, the sublime, Tuckerman reveals himself as a realist with a "hard awareness of human limitations." He finds the poet a better observer of nature than a meditator on life, but when Tuckerman fuses his observations with his meditations, Howe notes a strong upsurge of emotional vitality. He quotes generously from Sonnet VII, Part I, and from Sonnet XVIII, Part III. Sonnet X, Part I, is quoted in its entirety because he considers it "one of the lovelier sonnets" which illustrates "Tuckerman's high meditative eloquence." Turning to *The Cricket*, Howe is unable to find in it justification for Winters's high praise. He admits that it contains memorable passages but feels that these are overshadowed by stylistic lapses.

The rediscovery of Tuckerman in the twentieth century leads to some generalizations about his position at the present time. Running steadily through the critical writings mentioned is the complaint that the work is too frequently marred to permit him to be in the first rank of poets. A second recurrent observation is that, in the midst of dull verse, there are outstanding lines and phrases that label Tuckerman an intuitive poet. A third acknowledgement is that he is one of those poets who tends to baffle critics who, while recognizing the good in his poetry, are hard put to say much more than that it must be read to be appreciated. In fact, the reviews and notices are short and yet the writers felt so compelled to include complete sonnets and generous snatches that their reviews contain as much quotation and example as commentary.

When the choice of sonnets used by the various critics and reviewers mentioned is considered, it becomes clear that there is no onesidedness in selection. The reason for such diversity of choice is that the sonnets have general excellence. None far outshines the rest; the earliest are as good as the latest. Tuckerman is still too little known for his work to have settled into a conventional pattern. In time, no doubt, anthologists and literary historians will establish certain of the sonnets as representative of his best work; and constant repetition of them will impose its limiting effects—as has already happened in the cases of Walt Whitman and Emily Dickinson.

While such inevitable procedure usually prevents aggrandizement of other works, it is serviceable by making selected ones, by constant reappearance, well-known and familiar. Tuckerman has not yet reached this stage. Up to this time, the lack of concentration on specific sonnets tends to leave the impression that he is a perpetually rediscovered poet on the periphery of greatness. When the sonnets, *The Cricket,* and a few of the conventional pieces achieve a greater degree of familiarity, Tuckerman may be expected to move into the center of the circle of great American poets.

V *Contribution*

Critical estimates of Tuckerman's work began with a series of private commentaries by the New England and by the Knickerbocker coteries in 1860 and were followed by public notices both in this country and in England in 1863 and in 1864. In 1931 Tuckerman's sonnets received the attention of popular literary reviewers; in the 1950's and in the 1960's concentration of interest developed not only among critic-reviewers but also among influential scholars. Enduring results are likely through the impact of scholarship. Scholars in the 1930's failed to take advantage of the opportunities to study Tuckerman, but their counterparts in the 1950's and in the 1960's have recognized his contributions and have begun to examine them in depth. When such distinguished men of letters as Edmund Wilson, Allen Tate, Norman Holmes Pearson, Yvor Winters, and Mordecai Marcus appreciate Tuckerman's gifts, it is evident that his work has permanent value.

The emergence of Frederick Goddard Tuckerman from obscurity increases the wealth of American literature in the nineteenth century and, by adding one more excellent poet to its roster, enriches greatly the literary scene. But Tuckerman's contribution to American poetry must be determined by the worth of his sonnets. In them he has clearly demonstrated a remarkable power in handling of the sonnet form in a new and independent way that was unmatched by any of his contemporaries. Aside from his invigorating the form, he most successfully and gracefully delineated personal grief, sorrow, and anguish in a detailed, objective manner. By examining his thoughts and feelings with scientific objectivity, he dared to go far beyond the rather strict and decorous limits imposed by the restraining forces of his New England heritage. His work, while anti-poetical in subject matter, represented a sharp break with strong tradition; but, in a larger sense, it marked a departure from poetical regions once ruled over by such New

England poets as Bryant, Longfellow, Whittier, Lowell, and Holmes. These areas had provided a good harvest; but, perhaps unwittingly, Tuckerman was impelled to find still more fertile soil.

Although New England was rich enough to nurture his poetry, the natural world of western Massachusetts provided only the background and setting against which he wrote of himself, a subject with no geographical boundaries. As he progressed from modest beginnings and unsuspected strength to heights of poetic mastery, Tuckerman gave back to his native place much more than he had taken from it. In his sonnets, he re-created New England's nature in a rich and exciting way; by his genius, he transformed the ordinary flora of the Berkshires into plants and flowers which took on brighter hues and grander shapes. Without excessive liberties in description and without distortion of observation, he made the flowers live new lives as they became instruments for matching background with feeling and for providing correlation between the concrete and the abstract. This poetic feat alone is a great accomplishment.

When it comes to rating Tuckerman as a poet, the first impulse would be to compare him with other sonneteers; but to proclaim his greatness and to challenge comparison will lead nowhere. An invitation to measure his sonnets against those of the great Elizabethans, the best Romantics, and even the outstanding Victorians would be unreasonable because Tuckerman is not in the same range as Shakespeare, Donne, Keats, Wordsworth, or Tennyson. His true worth can be judged only by weighing his work with that of poets of relative merit. If he is to be measured—as he ought to be—with his American contemporaries, there is no problem; there is no sonneteer of comparable stature.

The sonnets of Longfellow, Jones Very, and Bryant belong to a generation with which Tuckerman was poetically out of touch. All three New Englanders were solemn, conservative, and controlled; Tuckerman is grief-stricken, bold, and impatient. Where Bryant is elegant, Tuckerman is graceful; where Longfellow is sedate and calm, Tuckerman is intense and fretful; where Jones Very is religious, vague, and general, Tuckerman is reverent, clear, and specific. In fact, Tuckerman belongs to another generation of American poets: his true contemporaries are Dickinson and Whitman. Like them, he unfettered poetry from bonds that had outlived their years of excellent service; like them, he wrote with more concern for subject matter than for adherence to established formal standards. Dickinson, Whitman, and Tuckerman are basically personal poets; and their personalities inevitably molded their poetry in such a way that its individuality is unmistakable. Their works need neither title nor name for identification. Their differences bind them together and make them the successors to a period of poetry that was fading.

In the vanguard of American poets, Tuckerman is a pioneer and inevitably stands alone. Strictly as a sonneteer he is an anomaly because he was working with a form that was rapidly falling into low estate. The strong structure of the sonnet had begun to crumble and he succeeded in shoring up and in renovating the edifice. But the critics, belonging to the passing generation and accustomed to the old forms, did not see the shape of things to come. As a writer of sonnet sequences, Tuckerman is especially alone. Almost two generations ahead of his time, he may now be favorably compared in this genre with Edwin Arlington Robinson, Edna St. Vincent Millay, William Ellery Leonard, and possibly Conrad Aiken.

Intellectually, Tuckerman was in the mainstream of American thought; but, poetically, he was adrift in a tributary which was moving in a new direction. His place in American poetry is founded poetically on the excellence of his sonnets as works of intrinsic worth and historically on his perhaps inadvertent contribution to a fuller realization and understanding of the forces which were at work as American poetry moved out of the greatness of the nineteenth century into the grandeur of the twentieth.

Notes and References

References to letters and to posthumously published poems not cited herein are among the Tuckerman Papers. For a detailed listing, see Bibliography. References to the sonnets are from Witter Bynner's 1931 edition and are referred to as "Bynner"; references to other printed works are from the 1860 edition of Poems *and will be referred to as "Poems, 1860."*

Chapter One

1. In addition, the list of recipients of presentation copies includes: A. Tennyson, Everett, G. D. Wells, Brownings (deleted by a single line), Wilson, B. Hopkins, E[dward] T[uckerman], S[amuel] P[arkman] T[uckerman], W. D. Sohier, Mitchell, G. B. P., Briggs, F. S. Stone, Mrs. S[arah] Tuckerman, Mrs. S[ophia] M[ay] E[ckley], Mrs. A. G. Higginson, Mrs. Dennison, Miss Ogle, and Lady A. Noel.

2. *Parnassus*, ed. by R. W. Emerson (Boston, 1880), p. 357. Tuckerman is listed in the index as "Frederic Gordon Tuckerman."

3. Walter Prichard Eaton, "A Forgotten American Poet," *The Forum*, XLI (January, 1909), 62-70. See also a revision of this article in Eaton, *Persons Penguins & Peppermints* (Boston, 1922), pp. 51-64.

4. *The Sonnets of Frederick Goddard Tuckerman*, ed. by Witter Bynner (New York, 1931). This edition contains the five sonnet sequences and a detailed preface in which Bynner relates how the new material was found. p. 19.

5. *The Oxford Anthology of American Literature*, ed. by William Rose Benét and Norman Holmes Pearson (New York, 1938), II, 1589.

6. *Amherst Student*, December 15, 1939. He further noted that the "sonnets, whose value have just been perceived, were not in the orthodox form, acceptable to nineteenth century readers. His lyrics, with their elaborate rhythms and ornate personifications, were more acceptable. . . . A meditative outlook and an austere melancholy characterized the works."

7. Van Wyck Brooks, *New England: Indian Summer, 1865-1915* (New York, 1940), p. 313.

8. Yvor Winters, "A Discovery," *The Hudson Review* (Autumn, 1950), p. 458.

9. Mordecai Marcus, "Frederick Goddard Tuckerman's 'The Cricket': an Introductory Note," *The Massachusetts Review* (Autumn, 1960), p. 34.

10. Mordecai Marcus, "The Poetry of Frederick Goddard Tuckerman: A Reconsideration," *Discourse* (Winter, 1961-62), pp. 69-82.

11. Edmund Wilson, *Patriotic Gore* (New York, 1962), p. 490.

12. *The Complete Poems of Frederick Goddard Tuckerman,* ed. by N. Scott Momaday (New York, 1965), p. xxviii.

13. Bynner, p. 22.

14. *Literary History of the United States,* ed. by Robert E. Spiller *et al.* (New York, 1948), II, 900. Williams, in the section "Experiments in Poetry: Sidney Lanier and Emily Dickinson," says

> . . . we occasionally find a few . . . who think poetically ahead of their time. In the seventies, for example, Frederick Goddard Tuckerman, recluse and dreamer, was writing sonnets and other verses which . . . exhibited this restless search for a new technique. . . . Did Tuckerman, like Emily Dickinson, divine that his audience had not yet appeared? One wonders, too, whether others, still unknown to us, were not experimenting; or even whether Lanier, Emily Dickinson, and Tuckerman may not in the long history of our poets have developed apprehensions more delicate than those of their conventional contemporaries. In any case, such as these were the heralds of the great changes impending in the poetry of America. (900-1).

15. Wilson, *op. cit.,* p. 493.

16. Bynner, p. 49.

17. Bayard Tuckerman, *Notes on the Tuckerman Family of Massachusetts and Some Allied Families* (Boston, 1914), p. 53ff.

18. Bynner, p. 46.

19. W. G. Farlow, *Memoir of Edward Tuckerman (1817-1886) Read Before the National Academy, April, 1887* (Washington, 1887). Also, *Dictionary of American Biography,* XIX, 42ff. Edward Tuckerman was a close friend of Emily Dickinson. When he died, she sent this note to his widow: DEAR ONE,—" 'Eye hath not seen nor ear heard.' What a recompense! The enthusiasm of God at the reception of His sons! How ecstatic! How infinite! Says the blissful voice, not yet a voice, but a vision, 'I will not let thee go, except I bless thee.' Emily." *Letters of Emily Dickinson,* ed. by Mabel Loomis Todd (New York, 1951), p. 370. This note is dated March 15, 1886, exactly two months before her own death, May 15, 1886.

20. *Grove's Dictionary of Music and Musicians,* ed. by Eric Blom (New York, 1954), VIII, 582. Also, Bayard Tuckerman, *op. cit.,* p. 164.

21. Bayard Tuckerman, *op. cit.,* p. 58. Little is known of her. She wrote some undistinguished verse, but had a lively interest in literary affairs. Her most famous association was with the Brownings in Florence. The collection of letters which passed between Mrs. Eckley and Mrs. Browning (in the Berg Collection, New York Public Library) do not mention the poet and are of no use in connection with his life and works.

22. Bynner, p. 61.

23. The family house still stands and is now owned by the City of Boston. Allen Chamberlain, *Beacon Hill* (Boston, 1925) has a complete story of this house. It has a magnificent spiral staircase, and in the newel post is embedded the ivory disc which proclaims the house unencumbered by mortgage.

24. Bayard Tuckerman, *op. cit.*, p. 66. There may be some deep-seated connection between Tuckerman's fear of the sea and of the drowning of F. W. Goddard. In "To The River" (*Poems*, 1860, p. 63) are these lines:

> Oh, might I plunge beneath the flow
> For one forgetful minute,
> And, leaving all my dreams below,
> Rise like a bubble in it,
> And sweep along to lose myself
> With all the current seizes;

In "The Stranger" (*Poems*, 1860, p. 89), the moon vanishes "like a worn-out swimmer."

25. Bynner, p. 52.

26. *Ibid.*, p. 44.

27. *Ibid.*, p. 100.

28. *Poems*, 1860, pp. 137-39.

29. *Ibid.*, p. 142.

30. Eaton, "A Forgotten American Poet," *The Forum* (January, 1909), p. 63. Also, Bynner, p. 23.

31. Bynner, pp. 24-5. Letter from Frederick, the poet's son, to Mr. Eaton dealing with personal recollections.

32. *Poems*, 1860, p. 49.

33. The full title reads: "A Sample of Coffee-Beans, sent to the author, with a request for a poem; or, *The Publican, the Peddler, and the Poet." Poems*, 1860, p. 106.

34. Peto. See Shakespeare's *King Henry IV, Parts I* and *II*.

35. Fine miniatures of Tuckerman and his wife are in the possession of Orton Loring Clark, Amherst, Massachusetts; these were reproduced in Bynner. The portrait shows a youthful poet. His face is sensitive—with large, dark eyes; a prominent nose; a small mouth; a long chin. His black hair is worn long, covering his ears and reaching to his collar. His portrait is signed "F. G. Tuckerman," followed by "Cam."

36. For details regarding the purchase of the house in Greenfield, see Registry of Deeds, Franklin County, Greenfield, Massachusetts, Book 40, p. 221. Tuckerman bought the house for $3,000 on February 13, 1847, from his prospective father-in-law, David S. Jones. *Vital Records of Greenfield, Massachusetts, to the Year 1850* (Boston, 1915), p. 228, lists their marriage date, June 17, 1847. This informa-

tion is taken from the records of St. James's Episcopal Church, Greenfield. p. 67.

37. According to the late Margaret Tuckerman Clark, her grandfather had an excellent telescope. She told me that it disappeared during the settlement of his estate.

38. I doubt that Tuckerman meant this literally. He probably used "forty" simply as an indication of a long time.

39. Bynner, p. 66.

40. *Vital Records . . . to the Year 1850* lists the death of an unnamed daughter on June 29, 1848. p. 123.

41. *Poems,* 1860, p. 26.

42. This Green River is not the same one about which Bryant wrote in "Green River."

43. Much of Tuckerman's wide reading is not reflected in his work. These annotated volumes clearly indicate that his reading and knowledge of poetry was very extensive. In documenting Tennyson's borrowings, he quotes lines or passages from Chaucer, Spenser, Shakespeare, Marlowe, Milton, Dryden, Pope, Thomson, Shenstone, Burns, Keats, Shelley, Wordsworth, Coleridge, Southey, Young, Swift, Byron, Otway, De Quincey, Scott. These unique volumes are in the possession of Mr. Orton Loring Clark. Alfred Tennyson, *Poems* (London: Edward Moxon, 1842) 2 vols.

44. Mrs. Margaret Tuckerman Clark related this story to me.

45. Tuckerman's annotated copy of Tennyson's *Poems,* I, 175.

46. *Ibid.,* I, 182.

47. *Ibid.,* I, 111.

48. There are a few other notes. "A Character" has this notation: "Dr. Whewell, I believe." (I, 44); "The Ballad of Oriana": "This ballad is taken in idea from 'Fair Helen'" (I, 61); "The Palace of Art": "There is an old poem by Hawes (1505) called 'the Palace of Pleasure' of which I have only seen a portion,—but which commences—

> "I looked about and saw a craggy rocke
> Far in the west, neare to the element;
> Upon the top I saw refulgent
> The Royall tower" (I, 136).

About "Edward Gray" he commented: "This ballad beautiful as it is resembles—Barbara Allen" (II, 180). "Will Waterproof's Lyrical Monologue" has a biographical note: "Cock Tavern. Fleet St. London. by Wm. Colnet. (very old) June 9th 1851" (II, 182).

49. The manuscript of "Locksley Hall" was presented to Yale University by Mrs. Margaret Tuckerman Clark.

50. After the appearance of the Ticknor and Fields edition in 1863, the reviewer in the Springfield *Republican* noted that Tucker-

man's particular model was Tennyson "with whom he has had the pleasure of a personal acquaintance."

51. Hallam Tennyson, *Materials for a Life of A[lfred] T[ennyson]*. (n. p. [1894?]) 4 vols. II, 152-53. Also, partially quoted in John O. Eidson, *Tennyson in America* (Athens: University of Georgia, 1943), p. 142.

52. Town Records, Town Clerk's Office, Greenfield, Massachusetts. The daughter's name is listed as "Hannah," but "Anna" was the name she used.

53. The commonplace book has three obituary clippings.

54. See Tuckerman Papers. Also, S. A. Golden, *Frederick Goddard Tuckerman: An American Sonneteer* (Orono: Maine University Press, 1952), pp. 64-66.

55. *Greenfield (Mass.) Gazette and Courier*, April 17, 1871. For details of the sale, see Registry of Deeds, Franklin County. Book 291, p. 44.

56. Margaret Tuckerman Clark, "A Hawthorne Letter," *The Yale Review XXIII* (Sept., 1933), 214-15.

57. *Greenfield (Mass.) Gazette and Courier*, May 5, 1873. "F. G. Tuckerman is quite seriously ill at his boarding place, the American House." In addition to the Greenfield obituary, there was one in the Boston *Globe*, May 13, 1873, that identified the poet as the "brother of Professor Tuckerman of Amherst, and Dr. Tuckerman, the musical composer of Boston."

58. Bynner, p. 25.

59. *Ibid.*, p. 33.

60. *Ibid.*, p. 33.

61. Jay Leyda, *The Years and Hours of Emily Dickinson* (New Haven, 1960), II, 132.

62. Francis M. Thompson, *History of Greenfield* (Greenfield, 1904), I, 609.

Chapter Two

1. Julian Hawthorne, *Nathaniel Hawthorne and his Wife* (Boston, 1893), II, 274-75.

2. Bynner, p. 121.

3. Bliss Perry, *The American Spirit in Literature* (New Haven, 1921), p. 117. Perry's discussion of Transcendentalists includes the last five lines of Sonnet XXVIII, Part I, to conclude his section on the conflict of understanding and reason. This mention of Tuckerman may well be the only one between Eaton's essay and Bynner's edition.

4. Mordecai Marcus, "The Poetry of Frederick Goddard Tuckerman: A Reconsideration," *op. cit.*, p. 75: "Tuckerman employs equally beautiful symbolism combined with a more impersonal narrative in two poems which form a double sonnet about two beautiful sisters,

Gertrude and Gulielma. In the first of these sonnets the sisters are established as symbols of physical and spiritual beauty respectively."

5. Bynner's editing is faulty. The final word should read *ends*, not *end*.

6. Among the Tuckerman Papers is a separate version of the Long Island sequence which is numbered one through four.

7. *The Complete Poetical Works of John Keats and Percy Bysshe Shelley* (New York, n. d.) Keats, "On The Grasshopper and Cricket," p. 33.

8. As quoted in Marjorie Hope Nicolson, *Mountain Gloom and Mountain Glory* (New York, 1959), p. 17.

9. Bynner discusses Tuckerman as a war poet: "Ten years after the Civil War he set down about the conflict two sonnets gravely concerned and gravely aloof: the first and second of the fourth sequence" (33).

Edmund Wilson, in *Patriotic Gore*, says, "I can find among Tuckerman's poems only one certain reference to the Civil War, in connection with a young countryman who has been killed in it. Mr. Bynner believes that two of the sonnets, though written a decade later, also refer to the war; but this seems to me rather dubious: the army of which Tuckerman speaks seems, rather, a tumultuous metaphor" (491). Wilson does not identify the single war sonnet, but it seems to me that he must refer to Sonnet VII, Part IV.

10. Yvor Winters, *Maule's Curse* (Norfolk, Conn., 1938), p. 142.

11. George F. Whicher, *This Was a Poet* (New York, 1938), pp. 198-99.

12. Ralph Waldo Emerson, "Nature," *The Complete Essays and Other Writings of Ralph Waldo Emerson*, ed. by Brooks Atkinson (New York, 1940), p. 42.

13. *Ibid.*, "Self-Reliance," *Essays: First Series*, p. 152.

14. *Ibid.*, "Nature," p. 11.

15. *Ibid.*, p. 10.

16. *Ibid.*, p. 26.

17. *Ibid.*, p. 29.

18. *Ibid.*, p. 17.

Chapter Three

1. The variant readings are:

> And all at once, as I have seen the rain
> When the whole Shower is swinging in the wind–
> And motioned like a mighty pendulum,
> And back & forth between the earth and sky!

> When the rain smites the earth & back & forth
> In movement like a mighty pendulum
> And the whole Shower is swinging in the wind.

The final form is:

> And all together, as I have seen the rain,
> When the whole shower is swinging in the wind
> And like a mighty pendulum urged and driven,
> Beat back and forth between the earth and sky.
>
> (Bynner, p. 119)

2. In this case, the octet is the final version.

3. Exactly how Tuckerman may have pronounced "root" is not known, but it may well be that he used the New England dialect, rhyming "root" with "foot."

4. Bynner, p. 144.

5. Bynner and Wilson both suggest the possibility of Tuckerman's invention of a private mythology. Bynner says, "Some of his seemingly classical references, while bearing the ear-marks of validity, are to persons and events that seem to have existed only in his own imagination" (18). In *Patriotic Gore*, Wilson writes, "It has been noted by W. H. Auden that the invention of mythologies is an American specialty. Washington Irving invented Rip Van Winkle and the legend of Sleepy Hollow in order to provide the Hudson Valley with folk-lore. Longfellow concocted an Indian myth by combining the already rather garbled legends in the ethnological writings of Schoolcraft. Poe invented the dark tarn of Auber and the ghoul-haunted woodland of Weir. James Branch Cabell created the kingdom of Poictesme with its mélange of all the mythologies. And one of the queerest features of Tuckerman's work is his habit of alluding, not merely to characters from Biblical or classical antiquity so obscure that one cannot believe they are real till one finds them in a concordance or a classical dictionary, but also to personages who cannot be found because their names have been made up by the poet. The most outrageous example of this is the sonnet about one Eponina, whom the poet produces from nowhere but refers to as if her story were as familiar as Antigone's or Esther's. . . . Here Manoah and Deborah are real, but who are the other three ladies with the improbable-sounding names? We sometimes suspect Tuckerman of cheating by inventing a name to fill in for the rhyme." Referring to the identity of Dagoraus Whear, Wilson goes on: ". . . we learn the identity of this author, whom the poet names in a portentous way but of whose work one has never heard and of whom one can find no mention. . . . Was Tuckerman being mischievous? I doubt it: I imagine that these unrecorded characters had really come to live with him in the solitude of Greenfield. Whether or not he had read about them was a matter of no importance" (491-93).

6. *Le Larousse Pour Tous* (Paris, n.d.), I, 591.

7. *Dictionary of National Biography*, XX, 1343.

8. Tuckerman, "G. D. W." in Tuckerman Papers.

9. Ovid, *The Metamorphoses*, tr. Horace Gregory (New York, 1958), pp. 154-55.

10. *A Classical Dictionary of Greek and Roman Biography Mythology and Geography by Sir William Smith*, Revised by G. E. Marindin (London, 1932). "Actaeus . . . (Ov. *Met.* ii, 720) i.e. Orithyia, daughter of Erechtheus, king of Athens; also called Actaea (Ov. *Met.* vi, 711)," p. 14.

11. *Larousse du XXe Siècle* (Paris, 1929) 6 vols. II, 154.

12. *Harper's Dictionary of Classical Literature and Antiquities*, ed. by Harry T. Peck (New York, 1896), p. 1001.

13. Bynner and Wilson both suggest that these are mainly inventions. Bynner writes, "And in the eighth sonnet of the final sequence, his homesick line written in the city and mindful of trees near a beloved country dwelling is compact, through inwrought words, of poignant connotations. . . . Involved in the rich sound of the concluding line is a combination elm and home, apple and opal, sycamore and mine: an apparently whimsical but really emotional use of words that Edgar Allan Poe might have envied" (18-19).

In *Patriotic Gore,* Wilson writes, "And it would seem that this dissociated poet also invented words, very much in the manner of Joyce. . . . The holm tree can be found in the dictionary; but the ople tree and sycamine cannot. I think that Mr. Bynner is in general correct in his explanation of this passage" (493-94). "Ople" and "sycamine" are listed in Webster's *Unabridged Dictionary,* 1890 edition.

14. Bynner, p. 157.

15. *Ibid.,* p. 62.

16. *Ibid.,* p. 101.

17. The Golden Yard is more familiarly known as the Golden Yard-Arm. I have been unable to identify the "nine moonstars."

18. Bynner, p. 53.

19. *Ibid.,* p. 157.

20. Emerson, *op. cit.,* "The Poet," *Essays: Second Series,* p. 325.

21. For an investigation into the use of flora in American poetry, consult Norman Foerster, *Nature in American Literature* (New York, 1923).

22. Bynner, p. 77.

Chapter Four

1. Appendix III in Momaday's edition of Tuckerman's poems is given over to a detailed discussion of editorial problems. Momaday attempts to arrive at a correct reading of *The Cricket* by examination of four variant versions which he labels, *Cricket 1, 2, 3, 4.* The appendix is practically valueless because Momaday was unaware of

the existence of another—probably final—version, for convenience called here, *Cricket 5*. In 1949 I examined the Tuckerman Papers at the home of Mr. and Mrs. Orton Loring Clark, Amherst, Massachusetts, and, at that time, had a photostatic copy made of it. This copy is still in my possession, but the provenance of the original is, at this writing, unknown.

The Cummington Press edition of *The Cricket* (1950) is not based entirely on *Cricket 1*; the fact is that Mr. Harry Duncan, the printer, used my photostatic copy of *Cricket 5*, and this use accounts for Duncan's need to list the errata. In his commentary on the Cummington Press edition, Momaday only alludes generally to the errata. For example, he cites line 50 as being defective because it contains "lost" instead of "dim," but fails to state that the Cummington Press did account for changing "dim" for "lost" in its list of errata. Further, Momaday complains about line 81, but he does not say that the errata recorded the change from "all the" to "the lost." He errs again when he states, "the editor of the Cummington Press edition was the first to bring 'perfect' into the text, though he brought it in by way of the list of errata." The fact is that *Cricket 5* contains the word "perfect" in the line in question; it reads as follows: "And perfect tears! and crowning vacancy!" Had Momaday known of *Cricket 5*, he would have had no editorial problem.

Witter Bynner had read *The Cricket* when he helped recover Tuckerman's unpublished works. At that time he considered it "attic poetry" and thought so little of it that he did not mention it in his preface to the 1931 edition. Letter to me, September 30, 1963.

2. In "A Discovery," *The Hudson Review*, Yvor Winters has recognized the excellence of *The Cricket*, but has given a reading which is much darker and more lugubrious than mine. By calling it a meditation on death, he forces upon the poem a tight, orderly exposition of thought which it does not, in fact, have. It certainly lacks the meditative or contemplative qualities found in Thomson, Young, or Blair—or the serious moralizing found in Bryant and Very.

Marcus, "Frederick Goddard Tuckerman: A Reconsideration," *op. cit.*, p. 80, intimates that *The Cricket* is not essentially a meditative piece. He notes, for example, that "the cricket's song is a creative and soothing power because knowledge of death indirectly casts light upon the beauty and grace of existence, and because it imparts tenderness and resignation in the face of strife and loss."

Both critics agree that it is an excellent poem even though their readings are different.

3. *Poems*, 1860, p. 93.

4. *Ibid.*, p. 169.

5. *Ibid.*, p. 62.

6. *Ibid.*, p. 154.

7. *Ibid.*, p. 100.

8. Compare this line with the final one in Sonnet XIV, Part II, p. 84: "And simmering suds of the sea!"

9. Caÿster, a river in Asia Minor, is mentioned in Ovid's *Metamorphoses*, Bks. II and V. Gregory, *op. cit.*, p. 38, "Were singed with fires in the channels of Caÿster."

10. *Mythology*, ed. by Edith Hamilton (New York, 1940), p. 294.

Chapter Five

1. Compare "And the little wheels go over my heart" with Tennyson's line, "And the wheels go over my head" (*Maud*, Part II, V, i, l. 242).

2. Bynner, pp. 7-12.

3. *Poems*, 1860, p. 39.

4. *Ibid.*, p. 31.

5. *Ibid.*, p. 54.

6. *Ibid.*, p. 74.

7. *Ibid.*, p. 98.

8. *Ibid.*, p. 151.

9. *Ibid.*, p. 165.

10. *Ibid.*, p. 92.

11. *Ibid.*, p. 104.

12. These lines are in a fragment of a letter to an unknown correspondent. The excerpt reveals something of Tuckerman's problem in composing the piece; he writes, "The first six lines I have not touched, the 7th is perhaps an improvement,—8th—'dark blue scenery' I cannot improve, 'cascades' I do not like very well but I suppose may be allowed for rhyme's sake at least, 'Rustling' you disapprove of 10th. I retain this word because in the first place it suggested itself naturally, when listening to the 'soft cascade,' secondly because I find upon examination that Mr. Emerson has observed it, 'By Fate, not option frugal nature gave,/One sound to pine groves and to waterfalls.' "

Chapter Six

1. Julian Hawthorne, *op. cit.*, II, 274-75.

2. *Journals of Ralph Waldo Emerson*, ed. by E. W. Emerson and W. E. Forbes (Boston, 1913), IX, 318-19.

3. *The Atlantic Monthly*, April, 1863.

4. Jones Very had been his tutor during the freshman year at Harvard College.

5. The response from T. W. Parsons is only an acknowledgment of receipt of the copy and a promise to write again soon. The subsequent letter, if ever written, is missing. John Seely Stone, while not a literary figure, was an old family friend; his comment is sympathetic: "I know not whether the Sonnets, in particular, may be regarded as a sort of partial autobiography of their author, breathing out the broken utterances of a heart, crushed & sorrowing over the early death of a loved one:—but if they may be so regarded, be assured you have my tender sympathy, & my earnest prayers."

6. The British reviews cited are from the clippings in a commonplace book among Tuckerman Papers. See Bibliography.

7. *The Atlantic Monthly*, June, 1864.

8. Cited from clippings in Tuckerman Papers.

9. *Poems*, 1860, pp. 00-100.

10. *Ibid.*, p. 92.

11. Eaton, *op. cit., passim.*

12. Mrs. Clark supplied me with this information.

13. *Poems*, 1860, p. 36. In the text this sonnet is "Sonnet II." In a MS version, Sonnet I, "The starry flower, the flower-like stars that fade" has an epigraph, *"Sic itur ad astra."* An earlier MS has both sonnets as one poem of twenty-eight lines, entitled "Induction" and has the same epigraph.

14. For a detailed listing, see Bibliography.

15. This information was supplied by Professor Richard Cary, Curator of Rare Books and Manuscripts, Colby College, Waterville, Maine, where The Robinson Library is lodged.

16. These remarks are in a letter from Witter Bynner to me, September 30, 1963.

17. *An Anthology of the New England Poets from Colonial Times to the Present Day,* ed. by Louis Untermeyer (New York, 1948), pp. 477-78.

18. *Poetry of the New England Renaissance*, ed. by George F. Whicher (New York, 1950), p. xviii.

19. Winters, *Maule's Curse*, p. 125n.

20. Winters, "A Discovery," *op. cit.*, p. 458.

21. Marcus, "The Poetry of Frederick Goddard Tuckerman: A Reconsideration," *op. cit.*, pp. 69-82.

22. Wilson, *Patriotic Gore*, pp. 489-97.

Selected Bibliography

PRIMARY SOURCES

A. *Manuscripts and Letters*

The Tuckerman Papers, consisting of manuscripts of all the poems and many letters, are lodged in the Houghton Library, Harvard University, Cambridge, Massachusetts. They were presented in March, 1955, by Mr. Orton Loring Clark, Amherst, Massachusetts. A complete record of the Tuckerman collection as well as pertinent correspondence follows.

1. Manuscripts:
   (1) [Pocket memorandum book]
       A.MS.s.; [n.p.] 1830-1831. lv.
       Red morocco binding.
   (2) Poems
       A.MS.s.; Litchfield, England, 1854. 124f. (242p.) 8°.
       Tan sheep binding.
       Mainly fair copies, with some revisions.
   (3) [Poems]
       A.MS.s.; [n.p., n.d.] 53f. (106p.) 8°.
       Tan sheep binding.
       Rough drafts.
   (4) [Poems]
       A.MS. (unsigned); [n.p., n.d.] 79f. (18p.) 4°.
       Black cloth, black leather spine and corners.
       With a list of names, probably recipients of presentation
       copies of published book.
   (5) [Sonnets]
       A.MS.s.; Greenfield, Dec. 1872. 11f. (20p.) 12°.
       Wrappers.
   (6) [Sonnets]
       A.MS.s.; [n.p., n.d.] 33f. (63p.) 16°.
       Tan sheep binding.
   (7) [Poems]
       A.MSS. (signed variously); [v.p., v.d.] as follows:
       An Incident; [n.p., n.d.] 2s. (4p., comprising 2 complete
           copies).
       Rhotruda; [n.p., n.d.] 2s. (7p.).
       The Shore; [n.p., n.d.] 1s. (2p.).
       Poesy; [n.p., n.d.] 1s. (2p.).
       Gunhilda; [n.p., n.d.] 2s. (8p., comprising 2 complete
           copies).

     G.D.W.; [n.p., n.d.] 1s. (2p.).
     Lines written in the Blue Ridge, Virginia; [n.p., n.d.] 1s.
       (2p.).
     Nature and Necessity; [n.p., n.d.] 1s. (4p.).
     The Cricket; [n.p., n.d.] 2s. (3p., comprising 2 complete
       copies).

   (8) Journal, astronomical and meteorological.
     A.MS. (unsigned); Greenfield, 1847. lv. 4°.
     Marbled boards, black leather spine and corners.
   (9) [Scrapbook of reviews of his work]; [v.p., v.d.] lv. 4°.
     Green mottled boards, green leather spine.
 (10) [Commonplace book and scrapbook]; [v.p., v.d.] lv. 4°.
     Marbled boards, tan sheep spine and corners.
 (11) Wild flowers [a herbarium].
     A.MS. (unsigned); Scotland and England, 1851. lv. f°.
     Marbled boards, black leather spine and corners.

2. Letters:

From F. G. Tuckerman	To R. W. Emerson
From F. G. Tuckerman	To H. W. Longfellow
From S. M. Eckley	To F. G. Tuckerman
From Sophia Hawthorne	To F. G. Tuckerman
From Tennyson	To F. G. Tuckerman
From F. G. Tuckerman	To Tennyson
From F. G. Tuckerman	To Edward Tuckerman
From Tennyson	To F. G. Tuckerman
From R. W. Emerson	To F. G. Tuckerman
From F. G. Tuckerman	To Edward Tuckerman
From C. F. Briggs	To F. G. Tuckerman
From J. T. Fields	To F. G. Tuckerman
From N. Hawthorne	To F. G. Tuckerman
From S. Hawthorne	To F. G. Tuckerman
From G. S. Hillard	To F. G. Tuckerman
From J. H. Hopkins	To F. G. Tuckerman
From T. W. Parsons	To F. G. Tuckerman
From W. D. Sohier	To F. G. Tuckerman
From J. S. Stone	To F. G. Tuckerman
From Emily Tennyson	To F. G. Tuckerman
From H. T. Tuckerman	To F. G. Tuckerman
From Jones Very	To F. G. Tuckerman
From S. M. Eckley	To J. R. Lowell

American Literary Manuscripts. Austin: University of Texas Press,
1960. Has two entries on Tuckerman. One is a letter from Tuckerman, November 28, 1861, asking James T. Fields to change "deepens"

to "darkens" in "I took from its glass a flower." It is in The Historical Society of Pennsylvania, Philadelphia. The second is a listing of two manuscripts at the University of Texas. These are typed copies of "Margites" and "Refrigerium" and are of no use.

B. *The Printed Texts*

TUCKERMAN, FREDERICK G. *Poems*. Boston: Privately printed, 1860.

————. *Poems*. London: Smith, Elder and Co., 1863.

————. *Poems*. Boston: Ticknor and Fields, 1864.

————. *Poems*. Boston: Little, Brown and Co., 1869.

————. *The Cricket, printed from his Notebooks with permission of his granddaughter Margaret Tuckerman Clark*. Cummington, Mass.: The Cummington Press, 1950. Edition of 290 copies.

The Sonnets of Frederick Goddard Tuckerman. Ed. by Witter Bynner. New York: Alfred A. Knopf, 1931. Contains the first printing of all the sonnet sequences plus an excellent prefatory essay.

The Complete Poems of Frederick Goddard Tuckerman. Ed. by N. Scott Momaday. New York: Oxford University Press, 1965. The first such edition. Yvor Winters provides a provocative critical foreword and the editor has an interesting introduction dealing very briefly with Tuckerman and his relationship to Emersonian thought.

C. *Anthologies*

The following anthologies include selections from the sonnets and brief commentaries.

An Anthology of the New England Poets from Colonial Times to the Present Day. Ed. by Louis Untermeyer. New York: Random House, 1948.

Oxford Anthology of American Literature. Ed. by William Rose Benét and Norman Holmes Pearson. New York: Oxford University Press, 1938. 2 vols.

Poetry in English. Ed. by Warren Taylor and Donald Hall. New York: The Macmillan Co., 1963. This volume has no commentary.

Poetry of the New England Renaissance (1790-1890). Ed. by George F. Whicher. New York: Rinehart and Co., 1950.

SECONDARY SOURCES

A. *Books and Articles*:

BROOKS, VAN WYCK. *New England: Indian Summer, 1865-1915*. New York: E. P. Dutton and Co., 1940. Refers to Tuckerman as the "shyest of recluses"; describes the sonnets as "memorable expressions of tragic feeling" and "admirable in craftsmanship, firm, fresh and clear."

CLARK, MARGARET TUCKERMAN. "A Hawthorne Letter," *The Yale Review,* XXIII (September, 1933), 214-15. After a brief comment, there follows the complete letter dealing with Mrs. Hawthorne's offer to sell Wayside to Tuckerman.

EATON, WALTER PRICHARD. "A Forgotten American Poet," *The Forum,* XLI (January, 1909), 62-70. An appreciative article marking the recovery of Tuckerman in the twentieth century.

————. "A Forgotten American Poet," *Penguins Persons & Peppermint.* Boston: W. A. Wilde Co., 1922. A revision of *The Forum* article in more informal prose. The only addition is the inclusion of a letter from Tuckerman's son, Frederick, commenting on his father's poor eyesight and mentioning his reclusive ways.

GOLDEN, SAMUEL A. *Frederick Goddard Tuckerman: An American Sonneteer.* Orono, Me.: University Press, 1952. This monograph contains a biographical sketch, a consideration of the sonnets and of *The Cricket,* and a first printing of several posthumous poems: *G.D.W., The Shore, Under the Locust Blossoms, Poesy, Ode for the Greenfield Soldiers Monument* and excerpts from *Gunhilda.*

————. "Frederick Goddard Tuckerman: A Neglected Poet," *The New England Quarterly,* XXIX (September, 1956), 381-93. Summary and revision of material found in the monograph.

HAWTHORNE, JULIAN. *Nathaniel Hawthorne and his Wife.* Boston: Houghton, Mifflin and Co., 1893. 2 vols. Contains two letters from Tuckerman asking Hawthorne if he will accept a copy of *Poems.* Julian Hawthorne writes, "Among other of Hawthorne's correspondents . . . was a young poet, possessing his full share of the suspicious sensitiveness of the poetic fraternity, though not, perhaps, overburdened with genius. The two following specimens of his epistolary style will be found entertaining."

MARCUS, MORDECAI. "Frederick Goddard Tuckerman's 'The Cricket': an Introductory Note," *The Massachusetts Review,* II (Autumn, 1960), 33-38. Reprinting of *The Cricket* with corrections of errata cited and a brief comment stating that the reprinting is "a service to lovers of poetry and students of American literature."

————. "The Poetry of Frederick Goddard Tuckerman: A Reconsideration," *Discourse* (Concordia College, Moorhead, Minn.) V (Winter, 1961-2), 69-82. Comments on Sonnets VII and XIII, Part I; Sonnets I, XIV, XVI, and XIX, Part II; Sonnets IV, VII, XVI, Part V. Analysis of *The Cricket*—a sensitive and thoughtful study.

[TENNYSON, HALLAM]. *Materials for a Life of A[lfred] T[ennyson].* (n.p., n.d., [1894?]) 4 vols. Contains letter from Tuckerman to Alfred Tennyson defending *Maud.* II, 152-53. This letter is quoted in part in John O. Eidson, *Tennyson in America* (Athens: University of Georgia, 1943).

WILSON, EDMUND. *Patriotic Gore.* New York: Oxford University Press, 1962. Reprints Sonnets I and XXXVII, Part II; Sonnet XIV, Part V. Commentary on Tuckerman's work with particular notice to his use of allusions. "The phrasing surprises by its sharpness, by its individual flavor; and no feature of the world around him is too homely or too contemporary to be given a place in his verse." pp. 489-97.

WINTERS, YVOR. *Maule's Curse.* Norfolk, Conn.: New Directions, 1938. Tuckerman is "unquestionably a distinguished poet" and "is much like the Hawthorne of the last romances, except that he writes better." p. 125n.

B. *Reviews:*

BENÉT, WILLIAM ROSE. "Round about Parnassus," *The Saturday Review of Literature,* VII (February 7, 1931), 584. A favorable review. Reprints Sonnet VIII, Part III and Sonnet X, Part IV to encourage perusal of the sonnets.

EBERHART, RICHARD. "A Quiet Tone From a Rich Interior," New York *Times Book Review,* (June 20, 1965), 5. A brief but warm article, appreciative of the poet's inner resources.

HOWE, IRVING. "An American Poet," *The New York Review of Books,* (March 25, 1965), 17-19. A systematic commentary which calls favorable attention to the sonnets, but reserves judgment on *The Cricket.* The review is embellished by a caricature of the poet's portrait.

MORRISON, THEODORE. "The Sonnets of Frederick Goddard Tuckerman," *The Bookman,* LXXIII (March-August, 1931), 205-6. Review recognizes Tuckerman's intrinsic worth, but concludes it is better in "parts than in the whole."

REDMAN, BEN RAY. "Old Wine in New Bottles," New York *Herald Tribune Books,* VII (June 7, 1931), 12. A brief, tepid notice dealing as much with Bynner as an editor as with Tuckerman as a poet.

WALTON, EDA LOU. "A Neglected Poet," *The Nation,* CXXXIII (September 2, 1931), 234-35. An enthusiastic review. Praises Tuckerman very highly and reprints Sonnet XIV, Part II and Sonnet III, Part V.

WINTERS, YVOR. "A Discovery," *The Hudson Review,* III (Autumn, 1950), 453-58. Review of *The Cricket.* "It is a complex affair, but it is all of a piece, and the subject is fully and beautifully explored." Some commentary on the sonnets: "The two most beautiful, I believe, are numbers XVI and XVII of Part II."

"A Contemporary of Lowell and Whittier," (unsigned review) New

York *Times Book Review* (May 24, 1931), 12. An unenthusiastic review. The reviewer likes some lines, but has a low opinion of the sonnets as a whole.

"Book Notes," (unsigned review) *The New Republic*, LXIX (November 18, 1931), 26-7. A review lauding Bynner for printing the sonnets and, Tuckerman for his sensitivity to nature.

C. *Sources for Biography*

CHAMBERLAIN, ALLEN. *Beacon Hill*. Boston: Houghton Mifflin and Co., 1925. Information about the Tuckerman home at 33 Beacon Street.

FARNUM, CHARLES H. *History of the Descendants of John Whitman of Weymouth*. New Haven: Privately printed, 1889. Contains information about Anna Tuckerman.

KELLOGG, LUCY CUTLER. *History of Greenfield, 1900-1929*. Greenfield, Mass.: Published by Town of Greenfield, 1931. Vol. III.

THOMPSON, FRANCIS M. *History of Greenfield, 1682-1900*. Greenfield, Mass.: Published by Town of Greenfield, 1904. Vols. I and II.

TUCKERMAN, BAYARD. *Notes on the Tuckerman Family of Massachusetts and Some Allied Families*. Boston: Privately printed, 1914.

Records of Federal Street Cemetery, Greenfield, Mass. Now in possession of Dr. Philip Foster, Greenfield.

Registry of Deeds, Franklin County, Greenfield, Mass. Details regarding Tuckerman's purchase of house on Church Street, 1847, and its sale in 1871.

Vital Records of Greenfield, Massachusetts to the Year 1850 (Boston: New England Historic Genealogical Society, 1915).

Index

Index